ISBN: 1503016056
ISBN-13: 978-1503016057

DEDICATION

This story is dedicated to all the ordinary little girls who grew up during the war in many small towns throughout the country, and is written from that perspective.

CONTENTS

Acknowledgments   4

Prologue   5

Chapter 1 – Snow Time   8

Chapter 2 – I Know I Can Fly   22

Chapter 3 – The Blitz   31

Chapter 4 – The Lodger   40

Chapter 5 – The Picnic   45

Chapter 6 – Another Village   58

Chapter 7 – A Family   62

Chapter 8 – The Doll   65

Chapter 9 – Another Home   72

Chapter 10 – Home At Last   75

Chapter 11 – Our Gang   79

Chapter 12 – Happy Days   85

Chapter 13 – The Flicks   94

Chapter 14 – It's Over   98

About The Author   102

ACKNOWLEDGEMENTS

With special thanks to Peggy for all her help and continuous support.

Thanks also to Caroline Lawson of PC-Magic for her invaluable technical support and assistance, as well as her help in editing the second edition of this book.

Thank you too, to all the women who have shared their stories with me.

I would also like to thank my many friends and Ulverston Writers for their support and the confidence they have given to me when writing this story.

"Friends are the jewels in life's crown"

Lilian Wookey

**"Mists of memories swirl through our aged minds.
Fragile bodies deny our robust history".**

Lilian Wookey

PROLOGUE

Over the years, there have been many books, stories, publications and articles written about the terror and horror of WWII. There have been so many boys' stories written during those times, usually because they were so much more adventurous than the girls! Nevertheless, many different and unusual things also happened to us girls during the blitz in our small working class town.

This is the story of some of the ordinary, everyday working class kids who lived through those extraordinary times. Many of the names of places and characters are fictional, or have been changed to protect the innocent! It's not full of specific dates, and those that *are* there perhaps don't quite add up - after all, our memories of over 60 years ago could have faded a little!

So, a small town in northern Lancashire with a large shipyard and a population of around 70,000 people; a great history of proud, hard-working people. Our town! These tales are based on true happenings, warts and all (in fact, most of us kids did have warts at some time or other!). They're also about the women who, like me, are now in the autumn of their lives.

Both the town and its shipyard made major contributions to WWII, during which time local men and women worked long hours, both day and night, to turn out the big guns, destroyers, submarines, surface ships and all kinds of other armaments needed to help Britain and the Allies defeat the enemy. The local steelworks and ironworks companies also employed many workers, but not the thousands that worked at the shipyard (the main employer in the area).

Prior to the war, my Dad worked at the local paper mill.

The Paper Mill (Closed 1972)

Our town grew up around the shipyard and to this day, you can still see the order of hierarchy by the area, size and style the houses were built in. At that time, most working class people rented their homes, and my family lived in one in a long street of labourers' houses.

* * * * * * * * *

It is Sunday; Mam's cooking in the scullery, Dad's working in the backyard. The wireless is on. Mam and Dad usually shout to each other through the scullery door; today they are very quiet. I think they must have fallen out. The wireless goes off on its own. There is silence, then a posh voice starts to speak.

Mam shouts to Dad, "Quick! Fred, it's him". Dad comes in, listens, and walks towards the wireless. He turns the volume up to full blast. The man's voice booms out, speaking very slowly and seriously. I feel hungry.

"Can I have a jam buttie, Mam?", I ask.

They both turn to me and say "shush" together.

"Uh-oh", I think, "they look angry", so I shut up.

The posh voice sez, "We are at war with Germany".

Dad sez, "Jesus Christ! It's started; it's done!". Mam doesn't even tell him off. Instead, she slumps down onto a chair and leans her head on her hands, listening intently. Silent tears run down her face and Dad hasn't even shouted at her. He goes over to the wireless and leans on it. His legs look like they are sagging. I'm worried! They stare at each other, both saying nothing. The voice stops and there is another silence. Mam and Dad can't seem to move. I wonder if it is safe to ask for my buttie yet. I whine a little, "I need a drink".

Dad sez, "You're right. What we need is a nice hot cuppa". He goes over to Mam and puts his arm on her shoulders. "Come on lass, let's have a drink". Mam rises slowly, as if she has no strength. "A cuppa, yes a cuppa". She goes out to the scullery. Comes back in with our pretty white, china teapot and fills it with water from the big black kettle that sings away on the hook over our roaring fire. Mam looks at Dad; she is sniffing and sighing, and Dad passes her his large white hanky, "Here, blow ya nose. It's done now. We're all in it!"

She pours out our tea, puts two sugars in mine and Dad's, then cuts us a thick slice of the warm bread she has just taken out of the oven. We sit quietly at the table. I sip my hot sweet tea and all's well in my world. I have noticed the word 'war' mentioned, but it means nothing to me.

It's 11:15am, 3rd September, 1939.

I don't notice that word again until the autumn of 1940. On 13th September that year, nearly 300 incendiary bombs were dropped in an area not far from us, near where Dad works at the paper mills. All the adults are talking about how lucky we were. Until then I knew nothing about it. Thankfully, there has been only one casualty, sadly a small boy. Most of the incendiaries didn't go off, I expect that's why I didn't hear them. They were removed by the horse and cart full the next day.

The only time I listen to the wireless is when I sit at the table for tea, and Uncle Mac on 'Children's Hour' is playing. In almost every house, we kids sing along with great gusto to *"We Are The Ovaltines' Happy Girls and Boys"*. The war is never ever mentioned at either of those times.

* * * * * * * * *

The really bad blitz started in earnest around 13th April 1941, although there were three other bombs earlier that same year.

CHAPTER ONE
SNOW TIME

Tom wakes me up shouting very loud, "Mam, Mam, look outta the winder. What's happened?".

There is a curious glow through the thin curtains. Our Tom has jumped out of bed, drawn the blackout curtain then looked out. He's run through to Mam's bedroom. I'm too cold to get out of my bed but I can see through the winder where he has left the curtain open. It looks all white outside, with pretty icicle pictures traced on the inside.

I hear Mam say, "What you on about?" to our Tom. Dad shouts, he's mad at being woken up. "What the hell are you going on about? You know it's my day off! I only got to bed at two a-clock". He must have picked the alarm clock up because I heard him bang it down. "Bloody half past six! What the hell are you babbling on about?".

Mam sez, "Your Dad's been on fire duty our Tom, go back to bed and be quiet". But he insists, "Come and look our Dad, the snow is up to the winder ledge".

"Don't you exaggerate so much", Dad snaps.

"I'm not, honest. Come and look!" he protests.

I hear Mam getting out of bed, because the springs make such a noise. Then I hear her bare feet pattering over the lino. I want to get up to see what Tom's on about but it's freezing. Every morning when I get up, the lino is so-o-o cold, like walking in cold water without my shoes on and that makes me want to wee.

Our Mam gives a shriek, "Fred, come and look at this! Bloody hell, what are we going to do?". I hear Dad get out of bed.

"Bugger me, I've not seen it as bad as this before. Good job it's my day off. I'd never get to work in this". By this time I just have to get up to see what all the shouting is about.

"Oh heck Mam, what is it?". I look out to see the most beautiful sight I've ever seen and I'm nearly four! It's as if the whole place is bathed in a glowing white light and little white bits like stars are floating in the air. There isn't a single sound! You can usually hear the milkman rattling and clattering his bottles as he puts them on the step; brakes squealing as the paper boy stops to push the paper through the door. There isn't even his awful whistling. He only seems to have two notes, an in and an out whistle. It drives Mam and Dad mad. Our Tom can whistle properly, but Mam still has to tell him to be quiet cos he goes on and on! Now, no men talk and shout loud as they pass going to work, no feet clatter on the pavement, no coughing, no dogs barking. Mr Smith coughs very hard and loud every morning as he passes and then spits into the gutter. I know it's him because Mam sez he should be in hospital. Dad tells her he has too many mouths to feed. Mam swills the gutter every day where us kids like to sit. She tells us we could catch TB. I know I won't, I can't even catch a ball!

"It's lovely Mam, what is it?" I ask again.

"Bloody snow like I've never seen before", Dad swears.

"What's snow?" I'm so excited. "Are the stars falling out of the sky?".

"No it's just a bloody nuisance", Dad sez. I don't believe him because it's too beautiful to be a nuisance.

"Can I get up now?". Our Tom wants to go see what it's like outside.

Dad tells him, "you can wait till I've lit the fire. Go get back into bed".

"Or-r-r, I'll clear the ashes out of the grate if you let me come down", Tom wheedles. As no-one - not even Dad - likes that job, he wins him round.

"OK", he sez, "get dressed properly and put your shoes and socks on". It must be something awful because we usually just put our socks on to go downstairs. Not wanting to miss out, I wheedle. "Can I come as well?".

"No you can't, you can get in bed with me until't fire's lit". Mam doesn't need to say that twice; I love cuddling up to her in the big squeaky bed.

"Ouch, there's something sticking in mi bum", I moan as I snuggle down. "Move over", she sez, "that spring's a bloody nuisance, I keep telling Dad we need a new bed". I have a feather mattress on my bed and I sink right down into the middle of it, it's lovely.

Mam asks, "Do you need a wee, Jane"? I don't want to get out of bed, it's too cold, so I say "no". "Are you sure? If you do you'd better tell me right now. You know what you'll get if you wet our bed?" "I'll try", I say, knowing full well that actually I'm bursting, but don't want to get out of the warm bed. "When you get the po from under the bed be careful, don't spill it", Mam tells me. I crawl under the side of the bed and pull the po out carefully. It's a nice white china one with pink roses around the outside and a big rose inside on the bottom of it but now you can't see it. Mam puts smelly stuff in it every night before we use it, but it doesn't really help.

"Pooh, it stinks". I have to be very careful not to spill it.

"Shut up moaning and get on with it", Mam snaps, "then leave it out there".

I'm glad she sez that now I've had a wee in it as I think I might spill it if I push it back under the bed. By the time I climb back in my teeth are chattering and my feet feel like ice. I cuddle up to Mam. I can see my breath coming out like smoke does when Mam and Dad smoke a ciggy. I lie cuddled up to her and we both warm up a bit. My nose is freezing. I don't like to put my head under the blanket cos sometimes Dad pumps in bed, especially when he's been drinking beer. I put my freezing feet on Mam's legs. She sez, "Keep still, you're a bloody wriggler you are". She makes me laugh and I feel so secure!

I listen to the familiar noises downstairs. Tom is busy raking the ashes from our big black grate with the poker and making a lot of noise. Dad's gone to get some coal out of the coal bunker in the backyard. I can hear him pulling open the bolts on the scullery door. Then I hear him swear.

"Christ! Tom, bring me the shovel". Mam will tell him off again because that's a very naughty word.

Tom shouts back "What about the ashes?"

"Bugger the ashes, put them in the bucket", Dad tells him.

I hear Tom bang the shovel several times on the bucket; then hear him running through to see what Dad's found. I can hear him because he has big studs in his shoes to make them last a long time. They sound really loud on the flagstones in our kitchen. I want some studs in mine but Dad sez they're too big for my little shoes. He has an iron thing called a shoe-last; it's quite strange to look at. It has three things that look like different sized funny-shaped feet sticking out of it. He mends all our shoes on it. Mam sez he is good doing that, because we can't afford to go to the cobblers, especially our Tom, as he wears his shoes out quicker than anyone else she knows.

"What are you going to do Dad?" I hear Tom say.

"Dig us out son, that's what". He sounds shocked. "You go and get the fire going and then put the bloody kettle on; it's freezing in here".

Our Tom can do that because he's a big boy. Dad even lets him chop the wood for the fire with his really sharp axe. Not now though, because the snow has covered everything in our backyard. When I look out of the window, even the larder cupboard that hangs on the wall where we keep our meat, milk and eggs is covered with snow. Our Tom's quite a horrible boy; he told me once that he could push 15 cats into the small larder. I don't believe him. I can't lift the big iron kettle onto the hook that hangs over the fire when it has water in it. I'm glad really because it has thick soot on it and I always manage to get covered in it when I try to pick it up. Even Tom isn't allowed to take it off the hook when it's boiling.

Now I can hear Dad scraping something with the shovel. It's too much for Mam and me; we need to know what's happening. "Come on Jane let's go down, it sounds as if Dad needs me". She helps me to get dressed, puts her clothes on and we go downstairs.

"Oh bloody hell", Mam sez when she goes into the scullery, "What are we going to do?".

Dad looks at her and snaps. "Dig ourselves out if we can".

When Dad went downstairs and opened the door into the backyard the snow almost reached the top of it. It has all fallen into the scullery and he's trying to chuck it out with the little fireside shovel. I'm scared stiff, I think we'll be in here forever.

"What'll we do Mam? We won't have any food will we?" I'm shaking but more with excitement than fear or cold.

"Don't worry", Dad sez, "It isn't quite as high as it looks. It's what you call a snowdrift, up the door. I'll soon have a path through to the coal bunker and the lav, they're the most important things at the moment. Thank God I filled the coal scuttle last night".

After a while when the fire gets going, Mam pours the boiling water out of the big kettle. She makes us all a cup of sweet tea, then sez, "Here you are you two, sit by the fire to drink your tea".

"Thanks Mam", we say together.

The fire's roaring up the chimney, it's nearly burning my legs. I move them because some of the women in our street have big red marks on the front of their legs. Mam sez it's because they're lazy buggers and don't keep their houses or kids clean. They are always sitting up to the fire and that's what causes it. Sometimes they stand with their backs to the fire and lift their skirts up to warm their bums. They wear big bloomers down to their knees; they really stink then! It is a mixture of talcum powder, pee and sometimes moth balls. I don't want to be like them and Mam's always telling me off, she sez I am a lazy little madam.

Now we sit either side of the big brass fender that goes round the fireside. Mam puts black lead on the large black iron fireplace nearly every day to keep it shiny, and polishes the brass fender, so it always glows. The flames of the fire seem to dance along it. At each side of the fender, we have a pouffe to sit on, our Mam made them for us. Usually we have our hands and faces washed in the kitchen sink before we have our breakfast. Tom should be able to wash himself now he's nearly seven, but Mam sez he's allergic to water.

I think that we might not have to wash at all today, we'll both be happy with that! Still, it's bath night tonight. I love sitting in the big tin bath full of hot water by the roaring fire in the kitchen. It is lovely. Tom hates it! He thinks washing more than once a day is a waste. He carries on something awful when Mam scrubs him with carbolic soap. Mam sez how lucky we are to have a hot bath. There are notices stuck up all over saying we should only use five inches of hot water and I'm sure we get more than that. She tells us every time, "Tom has to have a bath to kill all the germs he picks up when he plays out".

There is one thing I don't like. It is after we've had our hair washed, Mam searches for biddies. She uses a biddy comb which has very tight teeth so it really pulls my hair especially if I have a tag in it. Our Tom's OK he has a very, very short haircut; Dad cuts it and then shaves right up his neck and the back of his head. When Mam dries our hair a bit with the towel, we have to sit with our head hanging over a newspaper. Then Mam starts to use the biddy comb - it seems to go on for hours and the skin on my head hurts. I dares'nt moan as I'm too near to Mam to duck if she goes to give me a clip on the ear. Luckily we don't have them often cos when we do, she takes twice as long. I can hear her cracking them between her thumb nails; it makes me shiver. When the school nurse comes to look in our hair, me and Tom don't ever get sent home. Some of the kids do - you can see the biddies crawling on their necks sometimes. They always come back to school with a pudding basin haircut, which doesn't look nice on the girls. We all call the nurse 'Nitty Norah, the Flea Explorer'.

Now Mam goes into the scullery and closes the door to keep the heat in the kitchen where we're sitting. We can smell eggs and bacon being cooked. A few minutes later she brings in a plate for each of us with a very special treat on - a fried egg and lovely, crispy brown fried bread as well. I dip one piece into my egg yolk and save the other so that I can dip it into my second cup of really sweet tea. It is my favourite.

"Get that down you both and you'll soon warm up", she sez as she puts them on our knees. This is unusual because Mam and Dad always make us sit at the table for our meals. Sometimes Tom wants to put his onto his knee by the fire. Mam always sez no and sez Nana told her, "the family that eats together stays together".

Today everything is different. Mam goes back into the scullery, brings in a hu-uge plate of two eggs, two bits of bacon and fried bread, and puts it into the large black oven which is part of our fireplace. Mam sez Dad has to have the bacon cos he works hard and needs to keep his strength up. When Dad cuts the crispy rind off his bacon, me and Tom always ask for it. Dad gives it to us and we chew it as slow as we can; it has a lovely taste.

Now Mam shouts, "Come on Fred, your egg yolks'll go hard". He gets mad with our Mam if they do that.

He comes in and sits at the table. "We're in trouble, lass", he sez.

"Why?" she asks, then sits down at the table facing him; she sez she doesn't want her breakfast yet. When she does that, Dad always sez she's watching her weight. I asked Dad once how you can watch your weight when you can't see inside yourself. He said, "That's what you do if you diet". I ask, "What does diet mean?". They always say I ask too many questions. Mam tells me though, "Dieting means when you don't eat as much food and you lose weight".

I'm glad she has told me that cos I thought it was to do with dying; and I don't want Mam to die. I know one thing: I'll never lose weight, I love my food! I think she's nice as she is because she isn't a great big lady like some of my friends' mams are. She is cuddly; I like to sit on her knee, although she won't let me very often. Dad doesn't want her to get thinner either. In fact he has shouted at her when she sez she wanted to diet and said he thinks she is looking for another man. Mam tells him he is horrible and jealous, and wishes she'd seen how jealous and bad-tempered he was before she married him.

Now Dad asks Mam, "Where's yours?" and she tells him she's not hungry yet. He looks at her funny. "Dieting?". She's mad at him, "if you must know, I've used all the bacon and eggs up. We can get some bacon tomorrow with our rations and you'll have to get to the allotment to feed the hens. There should be some eggs there with a bit of luck".

Dad swears, "Bloody rationing! What can you do with four ounce a bacon a week?" Mam looks at him, "The best I can, that's why you got mine. So is that OK then?". He doesn't say anything, and I'm glad because he frightens me when he shouts and makes Mam cry. Then he sez, "You asked me why we're in trouble?". He takes a swig of his tea. "Because I don't think I'll be at work this week. It'll take a week to clear this lot away and that's not saying we won't have more".

"What are we going to live on? If you don't go, you won't get paid", Mam demands.

"I don't bloody know!", Dad shouts, "if you're so clever, you work out how I can get there, and there's a lot worse off than us".

I don't like Mam and Dad shouting so I put my hands over my ears. "Stop shouting, it's naughty!"; that's what Mam tells us when Tom and me fall out.

Dad sez, "She's right! After all, everyone else will be in the same boat. We'll have a lot more than this to worry about if the shipyard can't get on with building the subs and destroyers".

Our Tom chimes in "And the big guns they build".

Dad nods, "Ya right son! This is one of the worst snowfalls I've ever seen in my lifetime! The wireless sez Morecambe Bay is frozen over, it's unheard of."

"Can we go to see it Dad?" Tom asks.

"How are we going to get there?", Dad shakes his head.

"On our bikes!". Tom's really excited.

Dad laughs, "Don't think so, we can't put skis on bikes".

Tom looks miserable, "Me and you could walk there, like we did in summer".

Dad pats him on the shoulder, "Sorry Lad, but it'd take us two days".

Piles of Snow in Dalton Road (Main Shopping Street)

The next couple of days, Dad's getting more and more worried. Now we have a big freeze as well. We are so cold in bed that we have to put all the old coats that Mam can find over our blankets. The inside of the bedroom window is so frozen I can't even scrape it off. One family in our street has had to take their curtains down to put on their beds. They still have to keep the blackout curtains up. All that is talked about now is that the snow has brought most of the industry in the North and the Midlands to a stop. Road transport is at a virtual standstill. The railway lines and tunnels are so blocked up they have to dig them out. Some people in villages near us are getting very short of food and their pipes are so frozen up they have to boil snow to cook with. I think that's a great idea! "Can we have dinner cooked in snow, Mam?". All she sez is, "Be quiet and don't be such a silly girl".

I shut up and listen. Mam sez kids should be seen and not heard. As they talk, I hear Dad say we need more ships and subs as the war is getting more and more dangerous. He tells us, "Some ships bringing in food have been sunk". He reads out loud from the newspaper, "Because there is no more imported food coming in, some of the dairy farms are being put to the plough". I have no idea what he means but it scares me anyway. He tells Mam, "Those buggers have a lot to answer for". I didn't know food came by ships, *I* thought we made it ourselves. I ask Mam if she thinks we might starve to death. She tells me to shut up whinging but she looks worried.

Our Tom sez to me, "I've seen a double decker-bus with snow up to the top of it". I don't believe him because I think they are as big as the ships in the docks. I've never been upstairs on one yet - I think my legs are too short - and Mam calls me a lazy little bugger and won't carry me. She tells me, "You're too heavy, now you're four you have to behave like a big girl". But I don't want to be a big girl yet! Our Tom always goes upstairs but most times the conductor makes him come back down because he doesn't behave – however, he doesn't misbehave when Dad's there!

"What's war, Dad?", I ask.

"Nothing for you to worry about", he pats my head.

"OK", I answer. I'm too busy getting ready to go out to play in the snow to worry about anything else.

* * * * * * * * *

Mam puts on my coat and wellies, wraps me up with a big scarf of Dad's around my neck, crosses it across my chest and puts it under my arms, then fastens it with a great big safety pin in the back. Nana has just knitted me a new pink pixie hood - it has a little point sticking up on the top of it - and some mittens in the same colour. The mittens have a piece of elastic stitched onto the wrist part of the mitts so they can be threaded through my sleeves and across my back so that I don't lose them. Mam sez my pixie hood will keep my head and ears really warm, but not to pick snow up with my mitts on as they will get wet.

She tells us both, "You two are very lucky that your Nana has all this wool. It takes two of our coupons to even get a pair of gloves or a scarf". I don't know much about coupons, but I know we can't have proper hankies anymore. I ask Mam why and she explains, "To buy two hankies takes one point out of our Ration Book, as well as money. I can put the points to better use. Especially the way Tom goes through shoes".

Now we use pieces of an old sheet that Nana has hemmed around the edges for us. Nana has unraveled a lot of her and Grandad's old jumpers as well, and she lets me roll the wool up in balls. She tells me I'm good at getting knots out, with my small fingers as hers are very stiff and have lumps on them.

I'm so well wrapped up I feel like one of the mummies I've seen in Tom's comics. Mam tells me I shouldn't look at his boys' comics because they have horrible creatures in them; she knows I get scared easily and get on her nerves. But still Tom shows me the horrible pictures when she isn't there and tells me, "It's OK, you can't read anyway!". Then warns me not to tell or he'll put toads in the lav.

16

By now I can hardly breathe, but that's because I'm so excited. Our Tom has already gone out with a big shovel to dig a passage from our house. He has a grey balaclava and scarf on that Nana has knit for him as well. I laugh at him because he looks like a baddy as I can only see his eyes! He's put on his short jacket, wellies and long knee socks that he has pulled over his knees so there isn't a gap where his short pants finish. Mam gives him Dad's work gloves to keep his hands dry. Some of the other kids don't have a scarf and some of the boys only have a short jacket and shirt or jumper on.

The lads from No. 71 in our street are really poor. They have seven kids - three girls and four boys - in their house. Three of them are still babies so can't play out. The two smaller boys are lucky cos they have jumpers on that are so big they hang down to their knees, and the sleeves hang right down over their hands. That'll keep them a bit warmer! Mam sez everyone gives them hand-me-downs. She sez it's a shame there aren't as many for them now as we all have to wear our clothes for a longer time, because clothes coupons don't go far. When I ask why they are so poor, our Dad tells us that their dad is too weak to work. Mam sez to Dad "Aye, weak in the head but not in his nether regions!". I ask Mam what she means, "Where's his nether regions?". She tells me, "It's another town and don't be so nosey".

The oldest lad – Jack - has his dad's wellies on, but can't lift his feet up quick or they will fall off. One of his little brothers is four like me, and he only has a pair of boots, not even socks! But his short trousers are so long though they are nearly down to his ankles, so he has them tied up with a piece of string. The other brothers have wellies on. They're what they wear all the time because of the wet and cold. Sometimes they piddle themselves - well, lots of us do that! But they have really nasty red rings around their legs where the wellies have rubbed the skin off. Mam calls them to the door and puts some Vaseline on their legs; they shout and jump around and Mam sez sorry but they'll feel better later. All the neighbours try to do things for them because they are so poor. The women say their mam is simple; I think that's because she can't talk properly.

Some of the kids get so cold that their lips turn blue and they have big yeller snotty streams coming out of their noses. Lots of them have long tongues and they lick their nose so they have a nasty chapped bit on their top lip. The ones who can't reach, wipe their noses on their jumper sleeves every so often and it freezes, then goes hard and shiny. My tongue only just goes over my lip so I can't lick my nose; I asked Mam why. She told me I was born tongue-tied, and the nurse had to snip the bit that was under my tongue when I was a baby. She tells me she wished she'd left me tongue-tied because now I ask too many questions. Anyway, it makes me feel sick seeing them do it but doesn't seem to bother them. We all have a good time; everyone comes out with shovels and finally they make passages through the snow in our street. I love it because they're like tunnels to me. They're higher than most of us little ones, so are a lot of fun.

When Tom or me have really bad colds, Mam keeps us in and makes us soup; Nana sez chicken soup cures colds. Dad has chickens in his allotment. Now though, we don't have chicken soup often; Dad tells Nana the eggs are more important and she agrees with him. I love lying on the sofa in front of the roaring fire, eating a bowl of soup. Some times when it's a horrid day, I cough a bit, hold my head and tell Mam I feel poorly. It doesn't always work, but when it does I lap it up!

I try not to say if anything if I have a sore throat though because Nana told Mam to wrap one of dad's sweaty socks round our neck and it will go away. They stink! I always ask Mam for an Aspirin, then tell her it is better rather than to put up with that sock. Now Mam makes vegetable soup with meat called scrag-end, or with bacon ribs. I don't like scrag-end as much as the chicken soup. I love bacon ribs though, Mam gives Dad them for his dinner and we can have one each. Sometimes Tom gets an extra one cos he's bigger than me, I think it's not fair! They are really tasty and we suck the meat off until the bone is shiny.

Everywhere you go now, you see lawns and even the big parks dug up and turned into vegetable gardens. People are obeying the posters that are stuck up everywhere saying, 'DIG FOR VICTORY.' Dad already grows loads of vegetables on his allotment, and he takes good care of his hens. The snow and ice is so bad that we don't get our milk until teatime now. I don't complain, it's frozen and when the cream on the top melts a bit, it tastes lovely. In the summer, if you don't take your milk in very early in the morning, the birds have learnt to peck at the cardboard tops until they get to the milk. Then they have a drink of the thick cream, it makes people mad at them.

One morning I hear a bell clanging. "What's that?" I ask Tom. He goes to see and rushes back in shouting, "Mam, Dad, come out quick".

"Stop shouting", Dad tells him.

"No, you don't understand, you have to come and help, it's Mrs Platt". He sounds anxious. You can tell it's an emergency cos Dad shouts Mam to come down from upstairs.

"I'm busy!" she shouts, "Meckin't beds", but she knows if Dad shouts her it's important. She comes down right away. Dad follows Tom to the door, so do I. There's a big commotion going on.

"What's happened?" Dad asks one of the other men who's come out. He sez, "Old Mrs Platt has collapsed and the ambulance can't get near".

It's hard because our street's on a hill. But it's really exciting! There's a line of people passing her down the street on a stretcher. At the bottom of the street is the first ambulance I've ever seen. It's square and much bigger than Uncle Stan's car, with writing I can't read on it. Mam and me are watching from the step. Mrs Platt nearly slides off at one time. "Dear God, what are they doing?", Mam sounds worried. All I can see is a big lump under a blanket. I like her, sometimes our Tom goes messages for her; she always gives him a three-penny bit and a sweet if she has one. Sometimes she keeps him talking and he gets fed up and moans about it, he's always in a hurry! I wish I could do her messages. I think I will when I'm a bigger girl, I like talking so wouldn't moan. Mrs Platt is a very big lady; she can't walk very well and has a stick. When the weather's better, she sits on a chair outside of her front door and stays out all day. She is so big she finds it hard to stand up, so one of the neighbours goes in and helps her out. She keeps an eye on us kids, which is handy for our Mams, and there is always someone to make her tea and give her dinner. Her husband died a long time ago, and her two sons have been called up into the army, so I think she is lonely.

Now the neighbours are all out, shouting lots of instructions at the stretcher bearers. By now, Mrs Carr from next door is on her step; Mam has knocked hard on her door as she knows she would want to know what is happening. Mam tells her, "She's had it, she won't be able to stand all this. It's her heart you know. Broken it is, losing those two lads as quickly as she has; this sodding war!"

There's that word again, and I don't think I like war.

Mrs Carr shakes her head, "I knew it when I saw that first telegram boy at the door. Then another one only a month later! She won't be coming home". She stands at the door, her arms bare as usual; this time they are folded importantly. Mam sez, "Poor old sod, what a way to go. Let's hope she meets them both again, wherever they are now".

I never see poor old sod Mrs Platt again.

Me and Tom still can't go to school and it's great, Tom has a set of old pram wheels with a plank of wood on and a rope tied to the front to steer it. He calls it his pusher. He uses it for all kinds of fun. Now he has dug it out of the snow in the yard, and Dad and him have taken the wheels off to turn it into a sledge. He goes to all the old ladies and men who can't go out and gets their shopping for them. He also gets lots of halfpennies, pennies and he even got a silver three-penny bit off old Mr Jones. He's mean though and won't share any of his money with me.

People everywhere have dug the snow off the pavements or made paths through it; but still no horse and carts or cars can get through the streets. One day we go up to the park and there are loads of people with sledges going down the hill. A big boy that knows my Tom lets me sit in front of him and takes me down - it is like flying and I love it! When we get to the bottom I really fly and land up spread out in a heap of soft snow. Magic! I plead with him to take me again but he won't.

Snow Fun in the Park

Then one day some men with big lorries come to our street to take the snow away, they start to shovel it up onto the lorries. I run into the house and shout for Mam, "Mam, Mam, some men are stealing our snow!". She comes out and I think she's going to stop them but she doesn't. She sez, "Thank God, it's about time too" and tells me, "They have to take it away; there is so much it's taking too long to melt".

I moan, "Why are they taking it; where is it going to?". She asks one of the men, "Where are you taking it?". He sez, "Up the Abbey". I moan again, "That's too far!". Then she tells me off again, "You won't be happy when our fire goes out and you have no dinner. The coalman can't get his horse and cart up the backstreet to bring our coal". "Sorry Mam", I shudder and don't complain anymore when I think about our fire going out. All our bread is baked in the fire oven. What would we do without the kitchen fire?

Every night before going to bed, I love sitting by the roaring fire listening to *The Crazy Gang*; my Tom loves them. I love *ITMA*, *Tommy Handley*, and *Around The Horne*. We eat thick toast that Mam makes by holding a toasting fork over the red hot coals and then she lets us put our own homemade bramble jelly on - we collect the blackberries from around the Abbey in the autumn. Mam takes us and we have a picnic as well, it is really good. Then Nana makes us the most delicious bramble jelly.

Now we'll have to go back to school. We are disappointed, but I don't think Mam is!

CHAPTER TWO
I KNOW I CAN FLY

I feel the warmth of the bricks on my bum and back as I sit on the backstreet floor. Our street is long and narrow and up a small hill. We live near the top of it. I sit and watch the small amount of traffic going by while Betty is on my swing. It's best when the milkman or the coalman goes by with their huge horses and carts. The milkman's horse is my favourite, it has great big eyes and lovely long eyelashes. I think it's a girl cos it smiles and boys don't - they just laugh when you hurt yourself; well, our Tom does. Our backstreet has just about enough room for the coalman to come down with his horse and cart. We used to swing on the back of his cart when he wasn't looking. We don't anymore since Mary fell off and the wheel cut her ear off. Ugh! It was horrible, all mashed up and stuck to the wheel. Now she's only got one and she had to go into hospital for a long time to make it better. But it never grew back and now where her ear was it is all red and ragged. Her hair hangs down to cover it. Her mam doesn't put a hair-slide in that side. Mary is quite proud of it and shows it to all the kids; it's horrible.

This is my safe place and I feel happy. It smells of dust, brick and dog pee. It is my gateway to happiness. When Mam and Dad fall out I sit out here and think about being able to fly when I grow my wings. On Mondays, I like to sit on the floor and listen to Mam doing the washing; I hear her swishing and swashing the three-legged posser in the dolly tub when she washes the sheets. When she's finished that, she puts a dolly blue into the scullery sink full of cold water and rinses them. I can't understand how blue water makes the sheets look so white. Then she puts them through the mangle in the yard to get all the water out, finally hanging them out on our washing lines. The lines go across the backstreet and tie round the hooks that are set into all the backyard walls. Everyone washes on a Monday so the backstreet is full to the top with washing and woe betide anyone with a horse and cart trying to go down. Even the rag and bone man wouldn't dare. The sheets always smell nice when they go back on our beds, Mam starches and irons them so they are quite stiff and crackly at first, but smell and feel lovely.

Washing Day in Barrow Island Flats

If she's in a good mood, I try to help her with mangling, but I've never managed to get more than a corner of a sheet through. If they get tangled and stuck, I'll be in big trouble cos Dad has to sort the mangle out when he gets home from work and he gets really mad. I always know when Mam is in a good mood cos then she has *'Music While You Work'* playing on the wireless as she does her housework.

Whispering with my best friends, sucking a sweet together, playing tag with the boys, skipping and singing, *'Marshes' Sass, penny a glass, when you drink it, it goes splash!'*. We all love this pop when we are lucky enough to get a taste. What more could you want?! Now I'm lazily dozing in the warm sun, watching a line of ants that are dashing busily to and fro. They seem to go one way and then rush back again to where they started. I spit right into the middle of them, just a bit so as not to drown them, but two almost do. I gently put my finger into the spit and they stick to it. I blow them off into a safe place. I'm sorry I've upset them. I thought they might need a drink cos it's so hot! I rub the spit out with my finger so they won't be as worried, squashing a couple in mistake.

"Whups, sorry ants", I tell them. I might not go to heaven now so I say a prayer, "Our Father, sorry". That makes me feel better but I don't suppose it helps the ants. I say loads of prayers, I don't want to be sent to Hell and that's where bad kids go. Loads of people tell me I might go there if I'm not good. My Sunday School teacher tells me I have to be good every day and that I don't listen properly. It isn't easy! Lennie down the street tells us off when our gang knocks his door and runs away. He comes out and sez, 'Heavens above, you lot are bad". Mam always sez, "poor Lennie". I think that's because he wears lots of white face powder and bright red lipstick.

Actually, I wouldn't mind being an Angel because they are beautiful

23

and can fly. I think I will be able to fly soon. Every night I try to fly down the stairs, but I can only do it off the third step and even then it hurts. Our stairs are very steep wooden ones and I often dream that I have flown from the top to the bottom. In the mornings, I stand on the top and try to be brave enough to take off, but then I get scared. When I lie in bed thinking, I know one day I am going to be able to fly right down the stairs. Of course, that's when my wings grow properly. I try to look at my back in the mirror to see if they're starting but it is difficult as I'm too short.

I would have been upset and sorry a bit longer about the ants, but the big dog from down the road comes up and sits beside me; he is taller than me when he sits. I bet he's squashed thousands! I ask him, "Have they've crawled on your bum, dog?". Yuck! I wouldn't like that. I try to look under his bum but his big bushy tail won't stop wagging. He is scattering the ants all over the place. I wonder if dogs go to heaven! I'd like him to be there, cos he's so nice.

"Ants, they can bite you know, dog. My big brother Tom told me that and he's seven and a half. He sez they have hu-uge fangs". The dog doesn't seem bothered. I put my arm round his neck because he's my friend, and he gives me a big lick on my face. He is big and curly haired, and has a beard that always stinks. I think he is the kind of dog who - if he was a boy- would be scruffy, have holes in his pants, and wellies on, but always happy. What my Nana would call a scallywag. She sometimes calls Tom that. I'm glad the paint's worn off his fur, two of the lads from down the street had painted a stripe down his back with some green paint they'd found. He didn't suit it! He licks me again and I splutter, "Poohee!"; his breath stinks. Still, he's cleaned my snotty nose. I was feeling quite dozy before that but he sure has woken me up.

I decide to have a turn on my swing. My friend Betty is having her turn and she's been on a long time.

"My turn, I want my swing". I demand.

"Just another minute", she sez bossily.

I'm really mad! She is going too fast for me to stop her. So I spit as hard as I can at her. I miss, which makes me madder.

"Na-ne-na, missed me", she sniggers. I'd swear at her but Mam might hear.

"I'll tell mi Mam", I whine. "It's my swing so I'm boss".

She chants, "Tell her, smell her, put her in the coal cellar". She upsets me again.

"Anyway your mam is fat and stinks", I snarl back. I say it quietly so Mam can't hear or she might clock me again. It's true, she does stink! Mi Mam told me she couldn't help it when I told Mrs Wild that she smelt. Then she clipped my ear for being rude! But she does, and Betty knows it. All the kids tell her but she doesn't care.

"Ger off now", I hiss!

"Don't want to". She swings higher and higher.

My Dad put two big hooks up in our backyard door jamb and hung some thick rope from it. Then he burned two holes in a flat piece of wood with a red hot poker to make me a seat. He has tied the rope through the holes so I can sit on it. It was my very special new birthday present when I was four and I'm nearly five now. It's the best swing in the world. I can sit singing, swinging and talking to myself for hours. I swing so high I feel like I could touch the sky soon. Mam tells me off when she catches me going too high, she sez, "If you fall off that swing and break your neck, you can't come to the shops with me". I never do, so it's OK.

I'm always happy and contented out here except when the word 'war' is mentioned. In fact, the word 'war' makes everyone quiet and no-one smiles as much as they used to. The neighbours would sit on their doorsteps of a night all talking and having a ciggie. They'd laugh and shout to each other. Now they never do that because if the Gerries come over, they could drop a bomb or even shoot them. Dad sez that's why we can't even have the gas lamps lit in the street anymore, because of those 'bloody Germans!'

Anyways, my swing is the best in the world and I feel just like an angel as I soar high in the air. I really know I'm going to fly one day! I start to whine again, "Ma-a-am". Then I hear Mam give a loud scream. I don't think she can be mad at Betty cos she is always telling me off for not sharing. Betty doesn't wait to see and shoots off home. I run into the house to see what's the matter and, Mam's sat on a chair with a letter in her hand; she looks really angry but she's crying as well.

I ask her, "What you crying for, our Mam?".

"Because that stupid bugger of a Dad of yours has volunteered for the Army", she snaps. I still don't understand what's happening. I like to sit on her knee so I try to climb on her lap.

"Ger-off, I'm not in the mood". She seems mad with me! I've only seen her crying when her and Dad fall out and he isn't even here. So I try again and this time she lets me. She is making an awful noise, her face is all swollen and her nose is running; it drips on my shoulder.

"Yuck, Mam", I pull a face.

She wipes her nose and my shoulder with the end of her pinny.

"What does volunteer mean?" I ask. I think it sounds such a nice word and I wonder if I can do it too. Then our neighbour, Mrs Carr, rushes in.

"What's happened?" she asks, "I can hear you howling next door".

"He's going in the Army, he's volunteered, the bloody idiot", Mam sobs.

"He's a part-time fireman, he doesn't have to go, he'll be exempt", Mrs Carr replies.

Mam starts shouting at her. "Don't you think I know that? The stupid sod! He's deserting us!".

I don't know what Mam means when she sez Dad's deserting us. All I know is that I've never seen her crying like this before and I'm scared. Poor Mrs Carr doesn't know what to do. Mam has frightened her as well as me. She screamed and shouted so loud that when Mrs Carr heard her through the wall, she'd thought someone was murdering her. She has rushed in half-dressed and looks really funny. Mrs Carr is a big lady. She's old, I think! Now she makes me want to laugh, because she has no teeth in, metal curlers in her hair, and her thick Lyle stockings are hanging round her ankles.

"Where's your teeth--?" I start to ask.

Mam shakes me slightly and gives me one of her looks. I know what that means so I shut up. Mrs Carr's elastic garters are hanging over her slippers and I can see her bare legs. They are white and lumpy like a bowl of bread dough that Mam puts to rise by the fire. I'm dying to ask if I can touch them. I bet if I pressed my finger on one it would go in a long way, but I know I'd better hadn't try! Mrs Carr has three boys and two girls. Babs, her oldest girl, is one of my best friends. She's five and three quarters and I nearly am five. I follow her all over the place.

"Is Babs coming out, Mrs Carr?" I ask.

"Shush Jane", she sez sharply. I look at her; she never shouts at anyone, and never at me cos I'm a good girl. Mrs Carr wears a pinny that she wraps round her body and her big arms are bare; they look like a man's arms. I'm mad at her for shouting at me so I say, "You're fat....ouch!". Mam slaps my leg hard. I know I've gone too far so I just sniffle. I won't get away with anything else. Anyway, my Mam never looks like that. She is a pretty Mam and looks like a girl.

I find volunteering means Dad will be going away very soon. He is going to be a shoulder. It doesn't matter much to me as I don't see him very often anyway - he works in the paper mills full-time and is a part-time fireman so is out every night watching for fires. Mam sez that's why he doesn't have to go away. He isn't home much and when he is he's usually asleep. Mam never goes to work so is there whenever I come into the house. I always feel safe.

"Is Dad going to fight the baddies when he's a shoulder?". Mam sez I always want to know the ins and outs of everything!

"Yes he bloody well is and serves him right". Mam is mad at Dad, I can tell. "It's not *shoulder*, it's *soldier,* and you're not a baby so say it properly", she snaps. I don't say anything, I don't want her to be mad at me.

I tell her, "I've got to go to the lav".

She sez, "Go on and hurry up, I want to go as well".

I wander into the yard and sit with the lav door open because our Tom holds the door shut to scare me when he's here. He won't let me out if he knows I'm inside - I can't breathe and scream for Mam. If she hears me she runs out and clocks him on the ear, but he's usually too fast for her. Then she always shouts at me for being soft. She sez, "I've told you a million times, don't exaggerate so much. You know it's only a wooden door, and it is six inches off the ground and has a big space at the top". She keeps telling me that, but she doesn't hear our Tom telling me he's going to put big spiders and snakes and frogs under the door. Still I think now if I sit in the lav, I can practice saying the word *shoulder*. I love sitting in here I can sit and talk to myself for hours. Now I know I haven't got long.

"Shoulder, solder, shoulger", that's better, "shoulger", I say it to myself, not quite right though. I'm struggling but I don't want Mam to call me a baby. "Oh well", I think - the best thing to do is not to say the word if I can help it.

"Jane, get out of the lav, I'm dying for a wee". Mam shouts down the yard.

"OK, I'm done!", I shout back, pulling a piece of newspaper off the string that's hung on a nail behind the door. I go to wipe my bum, but it's a picture of a horse. I sit and look at it. It's a great big horse with a huge mane of hair. I like it too much to wipe my bum on it.

"Jane, hurry up". Mam's outside the lav door now.

"OK, just wiping mi bum". I fold the horse up and put him in my pocket for later. I pull another piece off and shout. "Mam, can you come in? I can't wipe it properly". It's easier if she does it, she doesn't miss.

Mam pushes the door open and sez, "You're a lazy little madam. I don't know what you'd do if I wasn't here". I didn't know then how soon it would be before I would have to learn to do most things for myself.

"Thanks Mam", I wheedle. "Just get out of here so I can wee in peace", she sez as she sits down.

I go through the scullery into the kitchen. There's a knock at the front door, it opens and Nana comes in. I run up the lobby quickly give her a hug; I love her loads! She pats my hair, and sez, "Give over you silly girl". I think Nana's shy! My little Nana is tiny and very round. She is very old, Mam sez she is nearly fifty! She always wears a black hat over her grey hair which is tied into a neat little bun, tiny black shiny lace-up shoes - her feet look nearly as small as mine - and a long black coat. When she goes to the Spiritualist Church or anywhere posh, she wears soft black leather gloves. Mam sez that's because she was very well brought up and had lots of money until she married Grandad.

He is stone deaf and a very bad gambler. I do know whatever a gambler is, it's a bad thing to be. I sit listening to Mam telling Mrs Carr all about it. Mam sends me out of the room when she talks to her about things she doesn't want me to hear, but I just sit on the stairs and listen. Mam tells Mrs Carr that Grandad has stolen all Nana's diamonds. Her father had brought them home from the diamond mines, and Grandad has lost them all at the Bookies. I know why Mam was so mad at him. She always tells me off if I lose things.

Nana's father worked in the South African diamond mines and only came home about once a year. Each year when he went back, her mother was always left with a baby; I think that was very kind of him! Nana, being the oldest, had to help her with them. Her mother finally went mad and had to be locked away, I don't know why and I can't ask Mam because she doesn't know I'm listening! Then Nana had to take care of them all. I hear Mam tell Mrs Carr that Grandad is a local champion cyclist. He bets on himself and makes sure the odds are good by coming second or third, right up to the final race. Then he puts all the money he can beg, steal or borrow on himself to win. Sometimes he loses and hasn't enough money to pay his debts. That's when he demands money off everyone. He comes to Mam and shouts very loud at her, tells her she has to give him money or some bad men will get him. Mam sez, "He's a nowty sod" to Mrs Carr, but not to him.

Now, Nana takes her coat off. She wears a pretty flowery crossover pinny like Mrs Carr's but nicer. She has on a white blouse so doesn't show her bare arms. She's posh! I tell her, "Mam's having a wee. I'll shout her". I go to the door but there is no need to as she is coming in.

"Mrs Carr sent one of her boys round with a message you need to see me", Nana sez to Mam.

"He's going in the Army, how does he think we're going to manage?", Mam shouts at her. I think she's very naughty as sometimes she shouts too loud at my Nana but she doesn't seem to notice. Grandad shouts all the time so I suppose she is used to it.

"Aye he's a thoughtless so and so. You won't do too well on Army pay". When Nana sez that, Mam starts to cry again.

"I know", Mam sniffs, "He won't get more than half he earns now". Nana pulls a little white lace hanky out of her pinny pocket and passes it to Mam.

"Why has he done it, that's what I want to know? Are you still not getting on?" Nana asks.

"Have we ever? I should have taken notice of his mother. She used to say to me, 'He's a good lad if he just learns to keep his temper in check'. What I should have heard is, 'he's got a nasty temper'".

Nana shakes her head at Mam. "Yes, but that's the way it is. He's always been a good provider for you and the kids. It is men's ways you know. Your dad is the same. He was never as good at looking after us as Fred is with you".

Mam gets mad with Nana. "Just because you put up with Dad being a bully and a gambler doesn't mean I will. Don't forget this is the 1940s. Wait till he gets in. I hope they send him out to where it's all going on".

Nan a shakes her head. "Now then, that's enough in front of Jane. You know I'll help you out as much as I can".

I'm not bothered really, I'm quite enjoying listening to them talk. "When's Dad going away?" I enquire.

"Why? What do you want to know for?" Mam snaps.

Uh-oh, I don't think I've picked the right time. "Don't know", I answer.

"What do you mean, don't know?" Mam's mad at me and I haven't even told her why I'd asked. I wasn't daft enough to tell her now. I just wanted to know if I can sleep in bed with her when he's gone.

CHAPTER THREE
THE BLITZ

It's my birthday - Friday, 2nd May 1941. I'm five now. Because Mam has to work she's letting me have my two best friends to tea on Sunday. Two days to wait! She tells me I can pick anything I like for our tea.

"Can we have fried bread, and jelly and custard?"

She laughs and sez, "Not everyone loves fried bread like you, you can have your favourite sandwich". So we have condensed milk sandwiches, they are my next most favourite and my best friends like them as well. We call them 'coni-oni sarnies'. Nana sez she will make me a cake but Mam tells her to bring me a jelly instead. We don't want to hurt her feelings but she makes her cakes with egg powder and not much butter, they don't taste good and are like rocks. So Nana brings jelly in a rabbit shape, she made it in a jelly mould, and a bowl of custard for us. When she brings it in we sing, *"Jelly on the plate! Jelly on the plate! Wibble wobble, wibble wobble! Jelly on the plate!"*. Mary sings *"Jelly in Your Belly"* and we all laugh. Then the three of us play *Blind Man's Bluff*. It's a lovely party. Nana has made me another ragdoll and Mam has made me a new dress; they are both lovely.

She also makes Tom play out while my friends are here because he torments us all the time. She doesn't see him when he gets me cos he's sneaky. When he kicks me under the table, I try to get him back but can't cos my legs don't reach. Mam can tell I'm trying to kick him cos I have to slide down the chair, and tells us both off. He goes all innocent and moans, "Weren't me, it was her". Mam always sez, "If you're going to kill each other, do it outside, I've just finished cleaning up". If I carry on crying, she tells me, "Keep on crying and I'll give you something to cry about. You're a mardy bugger you are". I know then I'd better shut up. As soon she goes out the room, Tom whispers "Mardy bugger! Mardy bugger!". "Shut yer gob", I whisper back and he kicks me on the leg just as Mam comes back in. I start to tell her, "Mam---". She doesn't see him do it and she tells me off, "Don't start, I've had enough". She's angry and I know to shut up. Still, I'll get my own back on him one day when I can fly and decide I'm gonna spit on his head! Anyway Mam promises Tom she will save some of the party tea for him. I hope he can't have any and try to get my friends to eat it all.

On the night of my party, Sunday 4th May, the Gerries come and frighten us to death. I wake up with a start and wonder what that terrible whistling noise is. Then there is a terrible bang and our house seems to tremble. I shake Mam, "Mam, Mam, wake up. What's that noise?". I have woken up, terrified, to one of scariest noises I've ever heard. Then the terrible wailing starts, and it goes on and on. I'm sure it's in the bedroom, our bed shakes. There are other sounds like I've never heard before. The whistling starts again, then more very, very loud bangs. Mam has already jumped out of bed screaming, and starts to pull me up and out of bed as I scream at the noise.

Mam, quiet now, sez, "I'm afraid they're bombs, love".

"Bombs?" I start to ask.

"Yes just get up". She's scared.

I can hear people shouting in the street. Through the walls, someone's screaming. Since Dad's been away I've been sleeping in Mam's bed. We have to get up very quickly. "Let's go downstairs, don't be frightened", Mam puts her arm round me. "I am, I can't shush", I tell her. My teeth chatter together so hard they hurt, and the noises get worse. There's another loud whistle then a thud and a terrible bang. The glass in the windows tries to explode. We have sticky tape all across them so the glass doesn't fall out and cut us. While we are on the stairs, Mam shouts our Tom. He's been fast asleep and appears at the door all sleepy and confused. He rubs his eyes as he asks, "What's happening?" Mam tells him, "It's the Blitz, come on you two, down the stairs and under the table". When we open the kitchen door, the room is black with clouds of soot. It covers all of us as she pushes the door. The blast from a bomb has made it fly down the chimney, and the whole room is covered in a storm of soot.

"I don't want to go in there", I whine.

"Get in quick", Mam coughs.

"Why?" I start to ask.

She pushes me in. "Because I said so, that's why. My God, what are we going to do?". She stands looking into the room like a statue; her blackened face starts to get white lines down it. I feel so sad.

"Mam don't cry, please", Tom and me are both crying and coughing now. As we stand looking, there is another big bang and I feel the house trembling with fear. She pushes us both hard, "Under the table you two. I'm getting towels to wrap round your face. That'll help!". The table's pushed up against the stair wall and it's lined underneath with metal. Mam has put one of the rag rugs she's made over the flagstone floor. It's for us to sit on so it isn't too cold for our bums. This is the only shelter we have and is supposed to save us if our house gets blown up. I feel safer under here but don't think Mam does as her bum sticks out a bit. She comes back in from the scullery and wipes our faces with a wet flannel. Our Tom is so scared he doesn't even struggle; he hates washing most of the time. She has wiped hers and we look really funny with big black eyes. Tom starts to giggle, so do I, then Mam laughs and we feel a lot better. She sez, "Come on, have a drink of water, then I'll put the towels over our heads". She drapes the towels over us and we have to hold them to our chests. I moan, "I can't breathe". She tells me off, "Yes you can, just shut up talking so much, pretend you're in a tent". She pats my hand and I feel better. We squeeze together. I'm so scared my teeth haven't stopped chattering and I've wee'd myself again.

Tom puts his arm round my shoulders and sez, "Don't cry Jane". "It's alright for you, you're a big boy but I'm only five", I moan again. "Yeh and I don't pee myself". He laughs at me, "Stinker, stinker", he goes on. I try to slap him but he stops me. Mam sez, "Shut up and behave, let's sing some songs". She starts to sing like Vera Lynn, "*I'll be seeing you in all the old familiar places...*". She stops and we all scream together as the house is shaken with a series of the most terrible bangs. Everything in Mam's china cabinet clatters and smashes to the floor as it falls over and the glass door breaks. All her treasured ornaments are broken, even her best teapot falls off the table. The noise outside is terrible, guns booming and chattering, planes roaring overhead, and more and more explosions. It sounds like the end of the world. We cuddle together as hard as we can, and after what seems forever it goes quiet; I've wee'd myself again.

Mam starts to cry. "How could he?"

I ask, "Who?"

She sez, "Your Dad leaving us now!"

Tom sez, "He had to be a soldier, Mam".

I pat her hand and sing a song from Sunday school, "*All things Bright and Beautiful*". It still sounds as if the whole world is blowing up around us but after what seems like hours, the worst of the noises stop. Mam crawls out from under the table, and asks, "Are you both OK?". She lights a candle to see that we are.

"Light the gas mantle", I can't understand why she hasn't.

"Can't, we have to keep it as dark as possible".

"Why?" I start to ask, then scream.

There's a terrible banging on the front door and we scramble from under the table. I scream again, sure the Gerries have come to get us. Even Tom is scared! Mam goes up the lobby to the door, "Who is it?", she calls out but there is no answer, just more banging. She opens the door, a little at first and then wider. We hear her say, "Oh God, Dad, you frightened us to death, come in". It's Grandad. He's come round during the air-raid to see if we are all right. Because Grandad's as deaf as a post, the bangs don't bother him. He's watched the action in the sky and knows how frightened we will be.

Grandad shouts, "What a dog fight!". I didn't know dogs would be left out in the night and I feel very sad. Then he tells us that he could see the German planes in the searchlights surrounding the town and there were Ack Ack guns firing at them. He sez he could see the Spitfires fighting, and that there are fires all around. The shipyard has been hit with incendiaries and landmines, and terrible damage has been done to the houses around us.

Bomb Damaged Houses, Hindpool

"Just came to see you and the kids are all right". He shouts so loud he makes my ears ring again. "Half the next street's down", he bawls, "now I know you're all right, I'm going back to help. The Home Guard's busy tonight, worst raid ever!". Grandad has his flat cap on and Mam asks, "Where's your helmet?". He sez, "Weren't enough to go round, give mine to Tommy, he's got six kids". She goes to the door with him and shouts, "Be careful, Dad". "Aye, I will lass and you mind those kids!". He slides through the door and disappears into the pitch black night.

I sneak up the lobby behind her and as she closes the door, I peer out. There are searchlights in the sky and I can see a big barrage balloon lit up by them. Then a very loud voice shouts, "Put that light out! Now!". It's a nasty voice and it scares me so I run back up the lobby. Mam only has the torch she used when Grandad called and it isn't on. She tells us, "It isn't for us, somebody must have let a glimpse of light out from somewhere and if the German pilots see it, they will drop a bomb there". I moan, "I don't like that man, he shouts too loud". Mam tells me off, "That man is one of a group of men and women who are very brave fire-wardens. They walk around in the Blitz so that they can help people if they are trapped in the bombed houses".

"Will we be trapped Mam?" Tom's scared.

"No love", she hugs Tom.

After the Blitz, 1941

Grandad has no sooner left when the horrible wailing noise starts again. Me and Tom fly back under the table but Mam doesn't. She sez, "Thank God, it's the all clear. It's over for now". She goes out into the scullery. I hear her striking matches as she runs the tap and puts pans onto the stove. She comes back into the kitchen and pulls down the clothes airier that hangs from the ceiling above the fireplace. She swears, "Bloody Germans, they will go to hell, all this soot!". She shakes the clean clothes that have been airing on it. "Here you two, come on out from under there", then shakes the cushions from the settee and gives a great big sneeze. We giggle again as we crawl out. "Come on, sit on here, and take your clothes off". We both sit naked on the settee. It's freezing! The fire went out hours ago and you can't light one when an air raid's on cos they might see the smoke from the chimney. Mam throws a rug over us, it stinks of soot, we both moan. "Just wait a minute", Mam snaps and goes back into the scullery to bring in a bowl of hot water. "Come on, you first", she sez to me. I stand in the bowl and she washes me down from head to foot and puts on my vest and clean nightie.

"I'm cold, can I have my liberty bodice on as well?"

Mam sez, "No, you'll soon warm up in bed". I am so glad we are going to be able to go to bed, I feel much better.

"Don't you piddle yourself again", she doesn't sound mad this time.

"I'm sorry, I'm scared".

Our Tom pipes up, "You're always scared" but Mam shushes him. She fetches his water as he objects at having to stand in front of me.

Mam sez, "Turn round, our Jane".

I moan again, "Tell him to turn round!"

Mam's mad at me, "Do as you're told or you'll feel my hand on your legs". I turn round quick.

Tom is washed and dressed in his clean pajamas, which are so short his boney ankles and wrists stick right out. Mam shakes her head, "Poor Tom, I'll have to see if we have enough points to get you some bigger pajamas". She goes back into the scullery and comes back in with two hot cups of milk. "Come on you two, you can drink your milk in bed". She picks up the candle holder and gives it to Tom. "Here, you carry this and I'll carry the milk".

"I want carrying", I protest.

"You're a big baby", Tom sez.

I start to whine, Mam looks at me and I know I've gone too far so I make for the stairs.

"Get into my bed, both of you". We don't need telling twice. We are so cold, the only way to warm up is all of us to cuddle together. Mam gives us our milk and we sit drinking it until she comes back upstairs, all clean again. She brings us two stone hot water bottles wrapped in old towels so as not to burn us, then gets into bed and we all cuddle together. She sighs,

"Come on kids it's four o-clock and we have to be up at seven".

In a few days, there is another particularly bad air raid. It seems to last forever. The bombs are falling even nearer to us. We can feel our table shelter shaking and between all the noises, we hear the shrapnel scattering down. Tom is dying to go out to get some. But it isn't until we come out of the house in the morning that we find out just how bad it has been. The top block of the next street to ours and two blocks along have been blown up. Lots of people have been killed.

Air Raid Destruction, 1941, Holker Street

Mam also tells us our lovely old railway station is nothing but rubble now. A large crane in the shipyard has been blown up and two of the fire watchers have been killed. Also, losing the crane is an awful loss to the shipyard and will disrupt the building of the ships. Tom went to have a look and sez the crane looked all sad, like a huge monster that had been killed. Then he tells me the men were blown off the very top and they might be in our backyard. I ask Mam to take me out to the lav when I need a wee.

She sez, "There's now't there, just get out and don't be so stupid".

I peer outside and I don't see a body. "Why won't you come?" I ask.

Mam sez, "Because! That's why".

By now I'm practically dribbling so I make a quick dash and slam the lav door shut. I keep my eyes shut in case the body looks at me over the top of the door. I know they can, cos I've seen 'The Curse of the Mummies' on the ABC.

I'm not allowed to go to have a look at what the bombs have done. Tom does, he sez that in one spot there is a mound of earth as big as a house. He tells me that there are bodies and bits of bodies sticking out all over it. Mam tells me something called an aerial torpedo has missed the shipyard and hit the houses. Tom thinks it isn't all bad because a bomb has damaged his school. No kids are hurt though, cos the Gerries came after school time.

Air Raid Destruction, 1941, Town Centre

The boys are happy; no-one can go to school for almost a month. Tom never goes to school much anyway, although Mam doesn't know. He and his friends think it is all a great big adventure. They make the bombed out houses their playground. The boys like to swap shrapnel and bullets at school. Tom sez that the church by the school had also been bombed and a street across the road has been flattened. One bomb has dropped right in the middle of a street called Hartington Street. The fire engine had gone racing up the street and disappeared into a big hole called a crater. I don't think anyone on it was hurt but I bet it looked funny! The bakery and the chemist's shop were also bomb damaged. There are horrible smells coming from the chemist's shop but they soon open again cos they were ready protected a bit with corrugated iron sheets. I can see the bullet marks where the Germans have fired their machine guns. Us kids can't understand why the Gerries would want to machine gun the chemist. Mam sez the chemist is as good as any doctor. You can go to him for a cure for anything. He had lots of lovely big green and blue bottles of all shapes and sizes on his top shelves, they looked like jewels. Now they are all gone, smashed in the air raid.

Tom likes to play soldiers with his friends all the time. The big boys make wooden guns and the small boys have sticks they collect out of the blitzed houses. Almost every time they play out you hear at least one grown up, shouting at them and saying, "You'll put someone's eyes out with that", but they never do. Most of the kids have little brothers and sisters, the boys have to take care of their younger brothers. A lot of their mams have babies at home. The big boys force the smaller boys to be the Gerries but no one wants to be the baddies! Many a little kid is tied up till his mam calls to him to come in for tea. Even then she usually has to go looking for him. Tom sez they are a nuisance and it keeps them out of the way of the bigger lads who are in the gang.

Bombed Out Houses and a Shipyard Crane

CHAPTER FOUR
THE LODGER

We have a lodger now called Mr Brown, and he lives in our parlour. Mam has put a single bed in and he has a chair and a table, given him one of our rugs and made us a new one. There are built-in cupboards with drawers at the bottom in an alcove for his things, but I wouldn't like to live in there.

Mam has had the chimney swept because we haven't had a fire in there since the war started. He is covered in soot and has a long flat brush that he pushed up the chimney and we had to go out to make sure it came out of the top. Now Mr Brown lights the fire, but he always looks cold.

I don't think Mam likes him cos she huffs and puffs when he's in the scullery to make his food. I think he's OK though cos he gives her some money every week. Mam's mad at him because she has heard that all the men that have come to work in the shipyard are earning double what the men in the services are; some are earning more than three pounds ten shillings a week! Mr Brown gives her five shillings for his rent and gas, but she makes him pay extra for the couple of buckets of coal he has each week. She's mad at Dad as well for going in the army to fight the Gerries; he didn't have to! She tells us she has to spend a pound a week on food, the rent is eight shillings, coal and gas is another four shillings, and our clothes cost her around eight shillings a week. It takes every penny of the money she gets from the Army and that's why she has to go out to work. Tom wears his shoes and trousers out so very quickly!

A lot of the kids at school are full of stories of how they have been sleeping in shelters all night, and I soon learn what shelters are. Builders come right down our backstreet and everyone has a shelter built in their backyard. Our shelter is built of bricks covered with thick cement and has wooden slatted beds round the insides. We cuddle together on them with blankets wrapped around us. It always smells.

"I'm not going to wee in a bucket", Tom moans.

"Yes you will, you can't go outside because you could get hit by shrapnel", Mam tells him.

"I'll wee out of the door, I'm not weeing in front of you lot". He's adamant. Our lav's only next door in the yard but we can't use it when the raids are on, it's just too dangerous. We have a bucket in the shelter to do it in. I don't care but Tom does. He's a big boy now. Mam holds a blanket in front of the bucket when Tom has a wee so that me or Mr Brown can't see him. Mam soon makes a kind of screen to hide behind out of our wooden clothes airier and a piece of blackout curtain. I miss our airier because me and my friends cover it with a rug and use it as a den when Mam is at work; we play house or doctors in it and now we can't, our Tom always spoils everything! "We'll make another big rag rug to put on the floor, you can help me", Mam tells me. I feel really important helping her. She has to cut lots of old clothes up into strips and push them through a material that looks like sacking, then knots them. She lets me pick the pieces out for her.

"Is this right, Mam?". I have to make sure they are the right colours. I'm very good at it really. I think I'm doing something very important; I just like to ask her so that she'll tell me I am a good girl. She usually sez I'm a fusspot. Mam makes the rugs really lovely, always with a pretty pattern.

"Look at this, Jane". She's found an old brass oil lamp. "It's better than candles". She polishes until it is as bright as the fender round our fireside. It makes it seem a little cosier but I feel sick with the smell of the paraffin. Still, it's a better smell than the bucket! I think sometimes Mr Brown uses it as well.

"It's not as nice as being in our bedroom, is it Mam?" I ask.

"No, Jane, but we'll probably sleep in the shelter most nights of the week, so you'll have to get used to it". She sounds worried. It's a very sad time.

Although I'm not supposed to be listening, I hear the grown-ups talking about people being blown up chimneys, heads lying in the street and all kinds of gruesome things. I have nasty dreams. They say that in about two months, over a hundred local people have been killed with the bombs. Lots more people have been injured. Mam tells us the hospital is full, and hundreds and hundreds of houses have been either damaged or completely destroyed.

When the air raids are on, our shelter shakes and rattles. I ask Mam if it's raining, as I can hear things showering down on the outside like heavy rain. "It's bits of shrapnel off the bombs, silly - can I go out?", our Tom always wants to collect the shrapnel. "Don't be so stupid, our Tom", Mam is quite mad at him. Still, he always tries to be first out of the shelter.

Tom is quite a shrewd boy and the other day, he brought a packet of tea home. "Look what I've got for you, Mam". Tom stuck out his grubby hand and proudly showed her the packet of tea.

"Where the hell have you got that from?", she shouts at him. I can't understand why she isn't pleased with him.

"Have you been knocking about with that Grant lad?" she shouts again.

"No, honest! I helped an old lady and she gave it to me", he protests.

Mam looks at him funny, "Hope you're telling me the truth", she shakes her head at him. I don't know why.

I notice when Mam opens the tea packet, she unfolds it to get every scrap of tea out of the corners. I don't care where he got it from. It is such a treat to have a hot sweet cup of tea and a piece of crispy bread, fried in lard for our tea. I smell the bread frying. Mam makes it perfect, crisp on the outside, just turning brown and red hot. I like to dip mine into my tea, it's heaven! We are only allowed one egg a fortnight now, usually fried with a slice of Mam's fried bread; a really special meal. My mouth waters at the thought of it. I don't know how but she manages to get extra eggs now and again, it's really lovely when she does.

When the all clear is given, we come out of the shelter. If it's dark you can see red glows in the sky. It looks pretty yet frightening at the same time. It upsets Mam, "Those poor people", she always sez.

"What poor people?" I ask. "The ones the bombs have fallen on, stupid". Tom always seems to know everything and still frightens me when Mam isn't listening.

He tells me again, "When I go looking for shrapnel, I find legs and things in the rubble. I might bring one home and put it in your bed". He knows the things he sez scare me to death and now I have to look under my blanket every night. "I'll tell on you, our Tom", I whine. He just laughs and sez "Mam won't believe you".

I am always glad it isn't us and that the bombs miss us. I dream every night that I find arms and legs in our backyard and I am so-o-o scared. I don't understand why the Gerries want to bomb us! Mam tells us, "Our town is a great shipbuilding town and a port, that's why the Gerries are coming nearly every night".

She decides to take me to the Regal pictures today. We see Nelson Eddy and Jeanette MacDonald and they sing *Indian Love Call*. I think I love

Nelson Eddy! Halfway through the picture it stops, the air raid siren going. A man comes on the stage in front of the film and tells us we have to get down into the shelter. Mam decides we should go home to our own shelter as it is only a couple of streets away. As we get to the top of the street, I hear a loud whining engine noise, then a chattering and banging. Mam pushes me and her down in a shop doorway. It is machine gun fire; we wait awhile after the plane passes and we hear it drone away. We get up and are both OK. Fancy a Gerrie trying to shoot at us, and…we didn't see the rest of the picture!

I listen to Mam and Mrs Carr talking about the air raids. Mrs Carr tells Mam, "The station's been blown to smithereens and the Coppernob has been badly damaged". We knew about the railway station, but now I'm really mad about the Coppernob. I love going to look at it, all shiny black and brass in its big glass house, such a lovely engine. People say there is never much about the bombing in our paper or wireless. The Government doesn't want the Gerries to know whether they have managed to do any damage. Still, everyone knows that when it sez on the wireless or in the paper that there has been a raid in the North West, that they mean us. The funny thing is now they don't seem to manage to do too much damage to the shipyard, most of the time it's to the surrounding houses. I'm always glad the Gerries don't know where we are. I know that if they find out they will take me away. Our Tom tells me they eat little girls for dinner.

I keep being poorly with my throat. Mam doesn't believe me at first and tthinks I like staying off school to be with her. I do - but now my throat really does hurt all the time. I have to go to see Dr Magill. He has a big red nose, Mam sez he drinks! He looks down my throat and tells Mam I have to have my tonsils out. I have to go to see a doctor at the hospital, and when we go he tells Mam I have to come in for an operation. I tell him I'm not! Mam sez she'll clip my ear if I'm cheeky again. I didn't mean to be cheeky, I just don't want to go there, it stinks!

It is horrible when I go into hospital. I am taken into a room and have a white nightie thing put on, it fastens at the back and you can see my bum. Then I'm taken into another place where there are giant men and women in white clothes with things on their faces. They lift me onto a table and stick something they call a mask over my nose and mouth. Then I hear them say they are going to pour some stinky stuff called 'chloroform' on the mask.

I wake up on a very hard bench, with my throat and head really hurting. I cry, then I'm sick. Someone comes and takes me to a bed and I fall asleep again. When I wake up, I'm thirsty so they give me some water to sip. Later, I have a lovely surprise - they bring me ice cream. Then I

43

have more ice cream later and it cheers me right up! Mam comes to the hospital the next day to see me, and in a day or two she takes me home.

Tom and me have to share the same bedroom again. Mam's started to go out of a night, and our Tom hates me being in with him. We have single iron beds that rattle when we move. He tells me more scary stories, and I am so frightened that I tremble and my bed rattles like mad. I whine, "Give over our Tom, or I'll tell Grandad", but he knows I can't cos Grandad doesn't hear me properly. Mam tells Grandad when Tom is naughty and he tells him off but whatever I say he always sez, "Good girl" then pats me on the head. Sometimes I say, "You just wait till morning our Tom, I'll tell Mam". Then he threatens to cut up my one and only rag doll that Nana made for my birthday. I'm sure he means it and as Annie is my most treasured possession, I know to keep my mouth shut. I lose her to him one day though.

"Hya what you playing?" I ask.

"Go away". These are kids from two streets away and I have always wanted to play with them although they are all older than me.

"Can I play?" I ask as they surround me.

"Not unless you give us somat". I think to myself, "what can I give them?". I catch sight of Tom's ball in the yard so offer them that.

"OK, you can play", the big lad picks it up. Then they start throwing Tom's ball to each other and I can't catch it.

"Come on then stupid", they keep laughing and pushing me.

"I want the ball back please", I say.

"No way, you give it us".

One of them pushes me over. Uh-oh, I am in trouble!

"No I didn't, I lent it you", I argue.

I didn't realise they wouldn't let me play with them and they would still keep the ball. The ball is as precious to Tom as Annie is to me so I don't blame him for taking Annie up onto the shelter roof and stabbing her to pieces. Once I get over the heartbreak, that is! I'm luckier than him because my Nana can make me another one. She is not as pretty as Annie, my Nana hasn't many coloured embroidery silks left for her face. Still I am

44

luckier than Tom. Our Nana can't make him a ball! I feel so guilty.

CHAPTER FIVE
THE PICNIC

Everything is different today. Mam has packed us a cardboard box each and I have a big label pinned to my coat with my name on it (I've been learning to write it so can read it now). There's Teacher! She's talking to all the Mams. I've been told to stand by Tom with our boxes. A lot of mams are crying. I feel like crying too, though I don't know what for. I was still more excited than scared.

We are all lined up in the schoolyard and Tom is in the next line to me. I poke him, "Look at those big buses outside the schoolyard. What are you crying for, our Tom? Are we going on a picnic today? Don't cry, it will be fun, won't it?"

Teacher comes over and takes my hand. "Come on Jane, you're going on the first bus".

"Come on, our Tom", I look back at Tom.

"No", sez Teacher, "Tom isn't coming with you, he's on the next bus with the bigger children".

"No, no, if I can't go with him, I'm not going". I stand stubbornly holding on to his arm.

"Now do as you're told Jane, or Teacher will get cross", she sez. I don't fancy this picnic at all. The mams are stood watching and crying. My nose is snotty, and I want my Mam to wipe it but she's had to go to work so Tom is looking after me.

"I want a wee, I want Tom, I want mi Mam", I howl.

As I come out of the schoolyard to the bus, I can feel the spray on my face from the cooling towers behind us and I smell the horrible smell from Case's Brewery.

Case's Ales Brewery Near the Town Centre

My face feels wet but I think its tears. I'm glad I can't hear any animals crying from the slaughterhouse round the corner today, I already feel really very sad. Nearly all the kids are crying when we get on the bus, even the teachers are. They are coming round us now being kind, wiping our tears and snotty noses. But I'm sitting on a wet seat and my friend Grace, who is sitting next to me, is wet as well. We seem to be going a long way - lots of trees, grass and big animals called cows. I've seen them in my book at school but I didn't know they were so big! I've seen grass and trees in our park, so this must be the biggest park in the world! Teacher sez this is called 'countryside'.

Now the teachers start to take one or two children off the bus every time we stop. I don't like this idea and think it won't be much fun, this picnic, not if we're not all together. Teacher has come for me and Grace now.

"Come on, you two little ones", she sez.

"Not me, I'm staying on the bus, I'm going home to mi Mam". I grip onto my seat.

"Now then Jane", Teacher sez, "I'll have to carry you off like a big

47

baby. You don't want that do you?"

"I don't care, I just want mi Mam, where is she?"

I'm shaking and my teeth are chattering, even though it's too hot on the bus. Grace is sitting there, silently crying. Teacher lifts me off the bus and sets me down in front of a huge man and lady.

"She'll be alright when she realises she has to stop with you", she sez.

"I won't", I protest, "I'm not stopping, I want mi Mam, I want Tom, where are they?". The huge man grabs my arm hard.

"Stop it, you have to stay and we have to put up with you and that's that!". He has a big red face and I don't know what to do. Grace is standing beside me, still crying quietly. Teacher gets back on the bus and it sets off, leaving us behind. I can see Miss Brown looking at us and she looks upset. The big man doesn't let go of my arm.

Now the lady gets hold of Grace. They take us through a big gate into a yard - which smells terrible! We hear a squealing noise that sounds like someone is being murdered. We're both scared.

"It's only the pigs", the man big man sez.

"Pigs?". Grace is worried.

"I'll show you", he sez. Well! They are so big. We have seen little ones in our book at school and they look nice, not like these monsters who are covered in mud. They live in some wooden buildings called pigsties. The smell is awful and makes you feel sick.

"Haven't you seen pigs like this before?" the big man asks. He sez, "Pigs are not nice mannered animals and if you don't have nice manners, we will have to put you in with them".

"Uh-oh", I think, "we had better be good".

Back across the yard is a pretty white house with a big curved doorway and a seat built into either side of the porch. Little do we know how many days we are going to be sitting there for hours and hours! The woman asks us, "Do you want to go to the lavatory?". We nod desperately. We've both had accidents already and feel very uncomfortable. We are big girls now, so feel embarrassed about our wet knickers. She takes us down a path to a big wooden door.

"In there", she sez. We push open the door and go in.

"What do we climb on, Jane?" Grace asks me.

I have no idea cos the lav is a big high wooden box. There are two holes in the top with a lid on each. This is new to us. We think it is a lav made for giants. No wonder the people are so big - they would fall down the holes if they were little like us.

"I'm going to wee on the floor, Grace", I say.

Grace - who is older than me - sez, "Jane, the people will be mad at us if you do that. I'll give you a bunk up".

"Bunk me up then", I demand. She does. I help her up the best I can by pulling her up with one hand. I have to hold on to the lav with the other or I might fall through the hole. She stands on the lids, which help a bit.

"Ugh, look down there Grace, our lav at home isn't like this one is it?". The holes are so big, we hang on to each other, scared we will fall in. The smell is as bad as the pigs, and there are big fat bluebottles flying around down in the hole. Sometimes, one buzzes on our bums and it makes us scream. We have to climb off the lav to get the newspaper to wipe our bums with, which is hanging on a piece of string tied to a nail on the lav door. It cheers us up a bit that we can both have a wee at the same time so we decide to always try to go together after that. Later, we often see the man at the back of the lav shoveling the stuff out and putting it into a hole with the horse and cow muck. This is one place we never go near; it smells worse than the pigs. He puts it on the fields and you can smell it as you pass by.

Mam hasn't come to get me yet and it's nearly time for bed. They take us upstairs to a little bedroom in the house. The woman unpacks our boxes. We go back downstairs and she cuts a huge piece of bread and jam and gives us a drink of thick creamy milk. It's delicious! Then she takes us back up to the bedroom. "Get ready for bed". She only speaks to us to tell us what to do. She leaves us to get undressed on our own. I cry, "Grace, I want mi Mam. I need Mam to put my nightie on, she always does it. And I don't go to bed without a wash".

Grace sez, "I'll help, I help mam wash my brothers and sisters". I remember she has two brothers and a sister who is only a baby. I feel better cos I know she'll know what to do so we go to bed without a wash that night. Grace cuddles up to me, I feel a bit better. Mam is sure to be here in the morning.

While we are here, our life rarely changes. The woman wakes us up and takes us down to the kitchen to have a wash. Grace whispers to me, "Its freezing", and it is! The woman has given us a bowl of cold water to share to wash ourselves in, but I've only ever washed my hands before. I say to the woman, "Mam always washes my face" but she just sez, "Well now it's time you did your own". I do my best. Me and Grace are scared stiff that we'll get into trouble if we don't do as we are told. I have no intention of being put in with those big fat pigs! We shiver with cold every morning though it's midsummer and really warm outside. The farmhouse is an old building with very thick walls. It never lets the heat in and always seems cool.

We get up at 6:15 every morning because the people have to feed the animals before they go to work in the fields. I think our yearning for home and our Mams is one of the reasons we are always so cold. We are never not afraid, even though we don't really know what we are afraid of. The people have a small girl of their own; she's just about able to walk on her own. The woman washes, dresses and smiles at her. The man and woman never smile at us. We would love to help with the baby but we aren't allowed to go near her. I touch her fingers and hair if they aren't there for a minute. She gives me a big smile. "What are you doing?", the woman's caught me and really shouts at me, making the baby cry. Now the man's come in and she's told him I've done it. "No I didn't", I try to explain to him but he is really angry with me. "You little brat, I'll skin you alive if you go near her again", he snarls at me. He frightens me so much, and I know I won't ever go near the baby again.

What we don't know is that they are forced to have us with them because of the war and they get billet money for us.

Once we've had breakfast - always a thick slice of bread, jam and a cup of tea - we have to go outside to wait for the school to open. The people leave us to wait there every morning. "Sit there and don't move until your teacher collects you...", the man points to the seats in the doorway, "...and these seats are where you stay until you're told to move". We don't really mind cos they are nice seats and we can play house.

"You be Mam, Grace, and I'll be your little girl". I like this game.

"Come here little girl and see the lovely birthday cake I've made for you". Grace is a lovely Mam.

"Oh thank you Mam, I'll be a good girl. Please can I come home with you today?"

"Of course you can, let's go and get the train now". It's the main game we play, day in and day out.

Sometimes I'm restless, "Come on Grace, let's go and play in the yard", I say but she's better behaved than me.

"No, sit down Jane, you'll get dirty then we'll be for it!" Sometimes I just *have* to play and won't take any notice of her. She always gets worried, but *I* don't.

Our school is a small one-room community hall straight across the road from the farm. There is one teacher and our class has about eight or ten kids in it. They are five to about nine or ten years old. Grace and me look forward to school as it's the one place we can look for warmth and comfort. Our Teacher only looks like a girl and is really kind to us. She comes in early, before school starts, and takes us across the road. "Come on girls", she sez, as she takes us across the road. She holds our hands and it reminds me of Mam. When we go in she gives our hands and face a quick wash, then gives us another cup of milk before the lessons start.

"Do you want to go to the lavatory?" she always asks as soon as we get there. "Yes please". We both try to hang on so that we can use the school lav. Miss mustn't like it too much as we always wait to do our jobs in it if we can. There are no blue bottles to touch our bottoms!

At twelve o'clock we have something to eat. "Time for lunch children", Miss calls out and then helps us kids unpack our lunches. She unwraps our slice of bread and jam. She gives a few of us half an apple each, even a piece of cheese now and again. All the class are given a glass of orange juice to drink. Teacher sez the government sends it to us to build us up because of the war. I drink it but it's thick and I think I can taste cod liver oil in it, I don't like it much. We lie down for a sleep afterwards on folding camp beds set up with a little grey blanket on. We love them!

"OK children, time to wake up". When Miss wakes us up, she reads a story and then everyone has to try to read some back to her. I enjoy this cos I'm doing well at reading. Three o'clock always comes too early. Teacher takes us back across the road to the farm and ensures we are sitting in the doorway before she leaves us.

"Do you need the lavatory, Jane?". Teacher knows I have started to wet myself again and am in trouble with the people about it. They have complained to her so she's trying to help me. "No thank you, Miss". The man and woman scare me so much when we do anything wrong that I do wet my pants. If we make a noise in our room, the man comes upstairs with a sack. "See this? It's to throw you out of the window if you make any more of your stupid noise", he growls. Mam still hasn't come for me, I don't know why.

One day, the postman comes up the yard. He's always here before we go to school and leaves his letters on one of the seats in the doorway. This time he has a parcel. He sez to me, "Who's got a parcel then, Jane?" He has a box all wrapped up in brown paper. "I bet it's from your Mam. But you mustn't open it until they come home". I sit nursing it. I shake it gently then let Grace hold it. Grace sez, "It doesn't rattle so it might be a doll". I think it might be sweets as well. "If it's sweets, I'll share with you and the people can have some for their baby. If it's a doll, I'll let you hold it", I promise Grace. I show Teacher it when she comes to pick us up, I'm so excited. This is one day when three o'clock can't come fast enough. I rush to my parcel when Teacher takes us back over the road. She sez, "Don't forget you mustn't open it yet". I had forgotten! I would have to wait at least another two or three hours. Still I can nurse it, I'm so excited and so is Grace.

The people arrive back. They pick up the mail and go into the house. The man opens the letters then my parcel. He calls the woman over. They both look at it, talk quietly together and then put the box on the dresser. I wait and wait but they don't say anything to me about the box. I know if I ask them what is in it, I'll be in trouble. We aren't allowed to speak to them unless they speak to us first. The parcel sits on the dresser for what seems a very long time to me. I look at it every night. I would look in the box if I was tall enough, but the dresser is taller than me. One day it is gone.

I ask, "Where's mi box?"

The man sez in his loud voice "It weren't yours".

I am so upset I say, "Yes it was, my Mam has sent it because the postman told me".

They say I'm being cheeky, but I'm not. I just want to know where my box is. I have got so used to it being up there on the dresser even if I can't have it, I want to be able to see it. To me now it is a part of home. I know I'm in trouble when the man takes his belt off, he smacks my bum, but it doesn't hurt like losing my box does. He sends me and Grace to our room, because she cries as well. "Never mind Jane, I'll tell Miss", Grace sez, hugging me better.

The day after the upset, Miss keeps us in after school. The people have complained because I can't tie my shoelaces. "I'm going to show you how to tie your shoelaces Jane", Miss sez. I have to practice over and over again. I get frustrated, and upset cos I struggle at first. She keeps us there until I can do it. Miss gives us another drink of milk and a very precious homemade biscuit. "There you are Jane, you see - you can do anything if you practice, you didn't need to get upset". Miss gives me a hug. So Grace tells Miss why I was so upset all day. She looks really mad and asks me what happened. "You see, I wanted my parcel - the postman told me it was mine. It was on the dresser and it went - the man said it wasn't mine. And then I was naughty and sed it was". I sobbed again. Miss cuddled me and sez, "Don't worry, I'll sort it out".

Miss waited to see the people on the farm to ask them what has happened. The man tells her he only threatened me with his belt because I was cheeky and bad mannered at the table. That is a big fib, cos we never sit at the table. He sez the parcel had come from my Mam but just had some knickers in it. Then tells Miss I pretend that I can't tie my shoe laces to be awkward. Miss sez, "That is not true, a lot of children her age have trouble with co-ordination". "Ok, I'll be a bit more patient. Now you're here come and have tea with us. You'll see how well my wife looks after them". We watch him smile at Miss. I don't know if she believes him but he's asked her to stay for tea. We have sandwiches with meat on, and apple pie. It is lovely and it makes us feel happy. The people talk to Teacher and allow us to talk as well. Of course, it only takes a small amount of kindness to convince little kids that all is going to be OK. We go to bed feeling much happier, and I am sure Mam will be here soon. But she isn't.

A big boy called William has come to live at the farm. He is 14 and has started to work for the people and goes off to work with them all day. So we only see him of a night and on a Sunday when the people take us to church.

"Come on girls", William is nice and plays ball with us in the farmyard.

"Hey you, don't thee scare't pigs", the big man looks angry.

William laughs. "Right boss, it's only a ball. These two little squirts can't do much damage".

The big man goes in and bangs the door. William crosses his eyes and makes us laugh as well. I tell him though, "Don't cross your eyes Will, my Mam sez they can get stuck like that forever". He just laughs and asks "Do you want to see a bird's nest in the hedge?" Then he takes us along the road to look in the hedgerows. He shows us birds' nests and lots of pretty flowers. There are meadows full of red poppies, blue forget-me-nots, daisies and glowing yellow buttercups that shine on your skin when you hold them under your chin if you like butter. There are flowers called foxgloves, tall and beautiful, with lots of trumpets down their stalks. We want to pick them. Grace went to pick one to take home. Will pulled her away with a shout.

"No, Grace". He frightens her.

"What's the matter Will?", she is nearly crying.

"They are poisonous", he looks at her hands.

"How can they poison me? They are only a flower", Grace argues.

"Well inside of them they have something nasty and you never have to pick them or you'll die. So promise me you'll never ever touch them, even when I'm not there". We have never seen Will look at us like this before, and we know he is very serious.

So we both say, "We won't".

"Cross your heart and hope to die". Will makes a big cross across his chest and we know he really means it. So we cross our hearts and chant. "*Cross our heart and hope to die*". There are big fat bumblebees humming happily in and out of with them though and *they* aren't dropping dead.

"Why don't the bumble bees die Will?" I ask.

"Don't know but *you* will if you touch", he replies.

Then he pulls off some leaves from a lovely bush with blossom that smelt heavenly but was very prickly he said it was where the birds nest. These are hawthorn leaves; he puts some in his mouth and chews them, passes some to us.

"Go on then, chew them, they're nice", he sez, "We call them bread and cheese".

I put one in my mouth and chew, "They don't taste like bread and cheese", I spit them out, "They taste green".

He just laughs, "What about you Grace?"

54

She's finishes hers, "I think they're OK, but aren't they poison?" she asks him.

"If you're really hungry they taste good as a sandwich".

I don't think I'll ever be that hungry.

Then he sez, "Hold your hand very still". I put my hand out and he puts a creepy crawler on it.

"Ger it off-- Ger it off!", I panic and go to brush it off; I hate creepy crawlers. Sometimes, I would see cockroaches in my friends' houses and they make me scared stiff!

"Watch it Jane, that's a ladybird", he laughs. "Look at it properly". I look at it and it's beautiful, it is a bright shiny red, with black spots.

"Now what you do is make a wish then blow it away", Will held my hand. I blew quite hard and its little wings came out from under its shell and whirred wildly as it flew away.

"I wish".

"No don't say it out loud or it won't work", he sez.

So I silently wish my usual wish. She still doesn't come.

As we walk along the lanes, he stops to show us all kinds of things. Grace went to pick a leaf and it stung her fingers. She gives a little scream and makes me jump.

"What's the matter, Grace?", I look at her fingers and they are lumpy and red. Will is picking some long leaves. He gets hold of her hand and rubs it with the leaves.

"Here that'll make the sting go away".

"What are you doing?" Grace asks.

"These are dock leaves and those nasty things you picked are nettles", Will tells her.

"What do they do?". I stand looking at Grace's hand.

"Have a good look at them, both of you. They will take the stinging away". Will stands with them pressed to her hand.

When Grace pulled her hand away, she smiled. "Look Jane it's nearly gone and it doesn't prickle as much".

I thought I'd have a go, so tried to pick a nettle but Will stopped me.

"Don't be silly Jane, it hurts and you're not as brave as Grace. Here taste this". He puts a red berry in each of our mouths and tells us they're wild strawberries. Then he shows us how to find them. I don't think the special taste as the wild strawberry bursts onto my tongue for the first time will ever be replaced. They are so good; I've never tasted anything like them. It is a treat in what we don't realise is a harsh life. He shows us a meadow with a beck in, we can take our shoes of and paddle in one part that is very shallow, there are golden flowers called marsh marigolds. Further up there are primroses, cowslips and violets, we haven't seen such pretty flowers before. We even look forward to the people coming home from the fields now Will is with them. Everything seems a lot better because he is here. He makes life a lot nicer for us. He takes us to see the pigs, even strokes them.

"Come on, put your hands on them", he lifts us up. This is really scary for us, but it takes some of our fears away. They still look fearsome to us but he's promised us pigs don't eat little kids. He also tells us the people will be put into prison if they let them.

One night when the people are in bed, Will comes into our bedroom.

"Which one of you wants to sleep in bed with me? I know you like cuddles".

We both want to, but Grace sez yes first. I'm sad - I want a cuddle so much.

Will sez, "You can come in next time".

Will put Grace back into bed in the middle of the night. He knows that the people won't like him being nice to Grace.

He woke me up and whispered. "Don't tell anyone and you can come to be cuddled next time".

We know we can tell Miss though, she has told us we could tell her anything and we won't get into trouble. So we tell her next morning when she comes to collect us for school; we think she would like to know how kind Will is to us. Instead she looks all upset, "Grace, has Will hurt you? What did he do?"

Grace sez, "Course he didn't hurt me, he cuddled me but he wee'd down my back and I didn't like that". Teacher looks all sad and angry and takes us to school early. As well as washing our faces she takes our vests off and washes us all over. It isn't what she usually does and she keeps giving Grace cuddles; I don't think she needs to wash me all over.

"I haven't been wee'd on Miss", I say. I don't like all the washing but I wouldn't mind some of those extra cuddles. After all, Grace has had cuddles off Will as well, and I feel a bit jealous. We don't go home from school today until the people get in. Miss and Mr Miles the Vicar take us home where they talk to the people. Everyone looks mad and Will looks frightened. We are sent to our room not understanding what all the fuss is about. The next day when we get up, Will isn't there and we never see him again. We miss him so much, he made things so much happier for us.

A few days later, the people pack Grace's box and put it on the seat in the doorway. They say her Mam is coming for her today. "Is my Mam coming for me as well?", I ask. They say, "No" and then leave. I cry and cry then I have a good idea. "I'll come home with you Grace". She sez "Yes". When Teacher comes we tell her our plan. Miss sez, "You can't go home with Grace but you'll be OK, I'll look after you". "No", I cry, "I don't want that, I want mi Mam and I want to go home".

Grace's mam comes into school after we have eaten our dinner and my Mam is with her. "Mam! Mam! I'm coming home as well?!" I yell. "No Jane, I've just come on a visit", she sez. Mam looks posh; she's always been a cuddly Mam but now she isn't the same. She looks like a film star on the front of the picture house at home. Her hair is rolled across the top of her head and on the back she has something called a snood. It's like a coloured net which holds her long dark hair. Her dress clings to her, she isn't cuddly any more. Mam is beautiful but I just wish she looks like she did before.

Teacher sez, "Can I have a talk with you, Mrs Walker?". Grace's mam is taking Grace home right away as they have to catch the next train. "Bye Grace", I hug her. I would have missed Grace more if Mam hadn't come, but I know she won't leave me here now, so I'll see Grace at school soon. Mam goes with Teacher to talk whilst I lie down to sleep with the other kids. I can't sleep. I wait for Mam to come to get me. She looks very angry when she comes back. She sez to Miss, "I'm staying to see these people". Me and Mam have to stay in the yard as usual, and Mam gets madder when she sees how long we've been left on our own every day. Even more so as she realises they had left me to wait for them on my own.

When the people come home and Mam starts to tell them off, the big man smiles at her. He sez, "Come in, have some tea and let's talk about it".

We have a nice tea, like we had with Teacher. "I've never smacked their bums, or threatened, or frightened them. She is saying that so you'll take her home. She's really homesick you know". The man sounds really kind. I don't think Mam believes him because she tells them to pack my clothes. So I'm going home at last! When the woman brings my box, Mam picks up the little girl's doll.

"Here, don't forget your doll", Mam passes me a ragdoll like Nana makes but I know it's not mine. "What do you call her?". I tell Mam, "It's not my doll, it's the little girl's". I give it her back. The woman gets my arm, "Come on, if you're leaving". The man picks up my box and goes to the door, "We're busy and can't hang around". Mam looks shocked.

By now, we are in the yard and the door is shut. We set off walking down the road. She tells me, "I'm sure that was the doll your Nana sent you". I don't want to go back so I tell Mam, "It's OK, I gave it to her she is nice". "When this war's over, I'll go back and give that woman a hiding", Mam sez. Now I know she's taking me home cos she believes me.

CHAPTER SIX
ANOTHER VILLAGE

"Why are we walking such a long way? Are we walking home? I'm tired", I moan.

"No, we are going to the next village to see the Vicar. It isn't far, so don't be soft", she snaps.

We finally get to the Vicarage and Mam is talking to Mr Miles. It can't be long before we go for the train. I don't understand what's happening. Mam and the Vicar have taken me to a pretty little cottage. Mam knocks on the door and a girl answers it. She smiles at the Vicar and sez, "Come in", but he can't stay. He sez, "Hah Helen, I've brought Mrs Walker to see you about Jane". Mam and me go into the cottage. I feel scared again though I'm not sure why.

"Would you like a biscuit, Jane? I've just made them", Helen asks me. I can smell the baking, "Yes please", I can't wait! It's the best home-made biscuit I have ever had. Nearly as good as the wild strawberries! She tells me to call her Helen. I like that name.

"Come with me to see my baby", Helen takes me into another room. The baby's fast asleep; she has pretty pink cheeks and a dimple in her chin. She reminds me of my doll Annie that I used to have at home; she's lovely!

Mam has a cup of tea and a biscuit, then sez, "Must go now, train'll be leaving soon". I immediately jump up, ready to go. She sez, "Not you Jane, you're staying here with Helen and the baby". "No!", I cry, "I want to go with you. Please Mam, don't leave me, please, please, I'll be a very good girl". "Don't be soft", Mam sez. "Helen's a nice lady; you can help her with the baby and have lots of her homemade biscuits, can't you?".

Helen puts her arm round me, "I'll take care of you". She's nice, but I want mi Mam. I tell her, "I don't like you and I don't like your baby. I don't want any more of your biscuits either". I beg, "Please-e Mam let me come home with you". Mam picks her coat up and sez, "She'll be all right when I've gone". She goes out through the door and closes it. But I'm not alright! I cry and cry. She doesn't come back though. Helen pulls me on to her knee and nurses me until I feel a bit better, I stop crying. I still don't understand why my Mam doesn't want me. If this is war, I hate it!

But it's nice with Helen, the cottage is very quiet and everything sparkles. It only has two rooms downstairs - a kitchen and a scullery - and two bedrooms upstairs. I have the tiny one, it has pretty sparkling white net curtains, at the tiny window and a deep window seat that looks out over the beck. The single bed has a pretty blue and white flowered bedspread over it, and a pillow case in the same material. On the floor, Helen has made a little pegged rug to match, even the candle holder is blue and white china. The kitchen is very comfortably furnished, and has two fireside chairs and Helen and I sit in them every night where we drink warm milk and eat one of her biscuits. Helen cleans it every day, like Mam does at home. The baby is really good, she never cries. Helen doesn't have any brothers or sisters and her mam and dad live a long way from her. She sez she has to go on a train to see them. I think that's why she has me to live with her. I like her and know now that I'm not going home yet, so settle down again. We sit together every night, and listen to the wireless. I hear *The Warsaw Concerto* for the first time.

"I like this music, Helen", I take a sip of my milk. Helen sits leaning back in her chair with her eyes nearly shut.

"I think it's wonderful", she sez with a gentle smile. "The first time I heard this piece of music was at a concert with my darling husband James. I still enjoy listening to it though now it makes me feel sad and lonely". I think she is going to cry.

I pat her on the arm. "Don't cry, Helen". That makes her smile a bit.

To cheer us up and make us laugh she changes the station and puts George Formby with his ukulele on. We sing along with gusto to his *"I'm Leaning on the Lamppost at the Corner of the Street"*. Then Gracie Fields sings my favourite song it is called *"Sally, Sally Pride of our Alley"*, but I've seen her picture and she isn't very pretty.

Vera Lynn always sings *"There'll be Bluebirds Over the White Cliffs of Dover"*. Everyone loves her. She is called the forces' sweetheart because she sings for all the soldiers, airmen and sailors; she makes Helen sad again. They don't make me feel the same inside as the Warsaw Concerto music does.

I have settled in and as we sit together and listen to the wireless, she shows me how to make pom-poms with the cardboard bottle tops off the milk bottles. I wrap wool around the outside, pulling it through the hole in the middle. She has to cut the wool and tie the centre for me as I'm not very good with scissors yet. I love to shake them in front of the cat; he soon pulls them to pieces but we make more. I have my glass of milk with one of Helen's biscuits, and life is fine. This is one of the best times for me. I don't feel lonely even in the night. Still, I want Mam to come to take me home.

"Come on Jane, we'll go to get some milk". Helen takes me to a farm. I'm astonished to see how it's collected. I've only seen it in bottles and big milk churns at the dairy near where I live at home. The man and woman had never let us in to see the cows milked. The farmer can tell how surprised I am so raises the cow's big floppy udder and squirts milk at me. It is disgusting!

"Come on lass, you can have a go", the farmer gets up. He lets me sit on his little three-legged stool to have a go at milking the cow. I squeeze and squeeze but nothing comes out.

"Yuck, I don't like the feeling on my fingers", I moan.

The farmer and Helen laugh. I give up, it feels horrible, and I'm sure the cow doesn't think much of it either. I think it's disgusting - until the farmer gives me a mug of the milk straight out of his bucket. It's all froffy, still warm and creamily gorgeous. The farmer's wife comes out to see us, she makes us take some fresh homemade bread and some butter that she has just churned. It smells gorgeous and I can't wait to get home.

They stand talking together though, and the farmer is telling Helen about a war ministry man coming to the farm. He laughs his head off and makes us laugh as he tells us. Still laughing loudly, he sez, "Couldn't find a thing wrong but he tried hard enough. Went to the big field; I said, 'Don't thee go in there'. He showed me his badge and said this sez I can go anywhere I want on your farm. I said 'OK do what ya want'. So he did, but when't bull turned up, he had to run like hell. He shouted at me to get it off and I told him 'show it thee badge'. Never seen anyone clear a hedge as quick as he did!". By now, they were all laughing so much that his wife was crying and blowing her nose on her pinny.

Helen thanks them both for their gifts as we leave. "Thank you both, you're so kind. I hope James and I are as happy as you two are after so many years together". The farmer laughs again, "Aye lass, but it's not always perfect. When I was courting tol't lass I used to think I could eat her. Now I wish I had!". His wife laughs so hard she is crying again. She picks a broom up and swats him with it. Helen and me can't move for laughing, although I'm not quite sure what I am laughing at.

"Helen, I'm here", I shout as I rush in from school to show her my drawing. She isn't in the kitchen or the sitting room so I go upstairs quietly, thinking she will be seeing to the baby. "What's the matter Helen, why are you crying?". Helen's sat on her bed, head hanging down, with her tears falling all over a piece of paper in her hand,. She looks up with a red and swollen face, like mine when I cry for Mam. The baby's lying beside her on the bed fast asleep. When I start talking to Helen, the baby opens her eyes, smiles and closes them again. This makes Helen cry even more. I don't know what to do, so I cuddle her like she does me when I cry for Mam.

"There, there", I say, just like she does to me. I pat her on her back. "It'll be all right". I say that cos that's what everyone tells me, even though I know whatever they say, it never makes everything all right for me. Helen's mam and dad come the next day. I hear them talking about the piece of paper. It's called a 'telegram' and has been sent from somewhere called the *War Office*. Helen's dad tells one of our neighbours that Helen's young husband James has gone down at sea. I think this must be her darling James, but I don't know why he has gone down to the sea. Helen's mam and dad are taking her home with them this week

"Am I coming with you. Helen?", I ask. Helen puts her arms around me and gives me a cuddle.

"I'm sorry Jane but I can't take you with me".

I push her away, "Please don't leave me, please-e, I'll be really good, I'll look after the baby for you", I plead. Poor Helen; I make her cry again.

"Jane, I have to leave you here, you can't come with me, there isn't room".

"I'll sleep in your room!", I plead, "Can't I come with you, Helen?". I have begun to love her. But she sez Mam would have too far to go to get me back. She leaves me when I am at school the next day.

However, while I am at Helen's, I made best friends with a girl at the end cottage called Mo'…Maureen really. She has black hair and always looks suntanned. She's quite bossy but I don't mind cos she knows a lot of great places to play in. She has lots of brothers and sisters and has to help her Mam a lot. Her Mam is always happy and kind, and makes the kids laugh a lot. Now her mam - Mrs Jones - has come to see Helen before she leaves. "Don't worry about Jane", she tells her, "She can move in with us. With my lot, one more isn't going make a difference". So I have to say goodbye again.

CHAPTER SEVEN
A FAMILY

I'm happy here with Mo and there's always someone in the house when we come home from school. It doesn't bother me that four girls share one big bed. It means you always have someone to cuddle up to. The only thing is I wee'd the bed the first night. I am so embarrassed. I haven't done it since I first moved in with Helen. Mrs Jones doesn't shout at me for it, she's just plonks us all on the floor, turns the mattress over, throws a sheet on it and we've all tumbled back in. She sez, "Never mind chuck, you aren't the only one to have accidents. I often have to turn the mattress over". Then she asks me if I want the chamber. I don't know what that is but it sounds like something I can wear so I say yes. I'm embarrassed again when she brings it in – it's a po! I know what a po is and it is *not* a chamber, but that's what she calls it. She's so kind though, she soon makes me laugh and I forget to be shy ever again while I'm with her.

It's a hot summer. Mrs Jones sez I'm as brown as a berry. I've grown used to playing outside without shoes, and my hair is longer and a bit straggly. Mam won't let it grow long; she has a thing about biddies. I like it a lot although it gets a bit hard to comb sometimes. Every week, we all have a bath in the big tin bath that hangs outside on the wall. I feel loved and happy.

Ours is the last in a small row of cottages facing a beck, which is a bright sparkling stream. It's not too deep where it passes our cottage so after school, it is heaven playing there. The water's as clear as a bell and shallow. It keeps us busy sailing leaves with old match sticks in as masts and trying to catch the little flashing minnows which shine blue in the stream. Luminous dragon flies skim over the water. I sit with the sun shining on my back, my feet dappling in the water. I couldn't be happier, except if Mam comes to take me home.

The cottage has no gas, so the oil lamps are lit of a night. Even when it's hot, there has to be a fire lit at some time of the day. The big black fire grate has an oven at the side of it. Mrs Jones wears a pinny all the time and always seems to be baking, mainly bread, in the oven. We run straight from the beck and into the cottage. The smell of fresh bread is heaven. Life is finally good. I'm still waiting for Mam but Mrs Jones squeezes me so hard when I'm sad and she is such a big cuddly lady, I lose my breath in her chest. Then she makes me giggle and I forget to be sad. I'll always remember that kitchen with its flickering lamps, the fire glowing and the wonderful smells.

"Bath time, kids!", Mrs Jones has a great big black kettle hanging on a hook over the fire and a large pan of water on the edge of the fireside. She gets a thick rag, wraps it round the handle of the kettle and staggers over to the long tin bath, pours it in then fills the kettle again. She repeats this again and again and also does the same with the pan of water. Then she pours cold water into the bath dipping her elbow into it to make sure the temperature is right. By now the kitchen looks like a sort of inferno with the steam, the flames of the fire and the flickering oil lamps.

When the bath is full enough, she sez, "Clothes off", and all four of us girls strip off. As we only have a dress and knickers on it doesn't take long. Four skinny brown bodies without a bit of shyness between us! We sit in the tin bath just once a week because it takes too long to fill it up more often. First in are us four girls, then the three boys. It's a bit hard on them as the water doesn't look so good after we've been in, although Mrs Jones puts a couple of pans of fresh water in.

At least every week, one of the boys or Mrs Jones sez, "Don't anyone of you dare to wee in there". We all keep our promise and none of us do. We laugh and Mo always sez, "Only you boys would do that". They do, as well, and standing up if their mam isn't there! I think they are lucky to have an extra bit cos they can wee anywhere. We come out of the bath scrubbed, smelling and stinging from the usual strong carbolic soap. Even our hair gets washed in it; we all glow. I don't know if it's health or the strength of the soap. We sit around the table with fresh bread hot out of the oven and milk straight from the cow. The farmer makes sure we have butter on our bread, a luxury that you only find in the country. Every week we girls go for the butter cos we know we always get a cup of warm milk. We watch the farmer milk a cow especially for us. Going to school is nice now and it's OK going home; everything is so warm and happy.

Of course it all has to change. Teacher comes into class and shouts my name. I go to the Headmistress' office and there is another lady there. I don't know her though I have seen her in the village.

Miss Smith - the Headmistress - tells me, "This is Miss Anderson; Jane, you are going to live with her".

"Oh, no I'm not! I already live with Mo". I stand there defiantly.

Miss Smith replies, "You can't stay with Maureen's mother, there isn't room".

"Yes there is. I'm already staying there!".

Miss Smith looks at me and tells me very kindly. "You are not allowed to sleep four in one bed, Jane".

Miss Anderson smiles at me. "When you come to live with me, you will have a room of your own". She doesn't look a bit like Mrs Jones. Her hair is tied back and she is skinny; she won't be able to cuddle me better when I'm sad.

"I don't want to live with you. I want to live with them. I like it and I love Mo and Mrs Jones and all my brothers and sisters". I know they aren't really my brothers and sisters but I so want them to be. "I don't want a room of my own, it will be horrible". I know I shouldn't be so rude but I can't help it.

"Well I'm sorry, madam, but you have to go home with Miss Anderson today, you can't go back to the cottage". Miss Smith sounds angry.

"Oh no not again", I think. But I've finally learnt it's no good arguing so just stand there till they sort it out.

Miss Anderson looks at me and sez, "Don't worry Jane, you can see Maureen at school every day and can still visit them".

Then she sez something that makes me feel a lot better. "I'll take you to see your brother Tom as well". I can't believe it, I haven't seen him since I got off the bus! What I don't know is that he is only a few miles away and we actually live in the same are; he's been put on a farm in the countryside. I think to myself, if I see him again Mam might come.

CHAPTER EIGHT
THE DOLL

Miss Anderson is very posh, it seems to me. When we enter her little house, she presses a switch on the wall and electric light comes on. I have never lived in a house with electricity before; it's like magic! It is very different at Miss Anderson's. I have a tiny room all to myself - it is so-o clean but it doesn't glow with warmth or the smell of fresh bread like Mrs Jones's does.

The tiny house is called '*The Lodge*' which stands at the end of a long drive. All along each side are lots of huge trees called a wood – it's quite spooky! I hold Miss Anderson's skinny hand when we walk down it and I don't feel safe. The trees close over the drive which makes it darkish. There are all kinds of noises, like branches snapping, things we can't see scuttering along besides us, even owls hooting. Sometimes even Miss Anderson jumps and I nearly wet my pants, she tells me off for being scared but I don't think she's all that brave either.

At the other end of the drive is a very big house with huge, dull windows that I can't look up at, as I'm sure I will see someone nasty looking back out at me. We are invited to visit the big house every week and have to knock using its huge, iron door knocker in the shape of a lion's head which makes a very loud noise. When we are let into its large hall, it has stairs that curve right down into the hall, and dark red carpet going up them. In the curve at the bottom of the stairs lives a large, flat, curved piano which Miss Anderson tells me is called a *grand piano*. I know why! It isn't a bit like the piano one of the neighbours in our street has at home, it's much posher! I ask can I play it, not that I can play real music but I like messing about. She tells me no and sez it isn't to be played again until the Captain comes home from the war. There it is again, that word, '*war*'...

On the days that we go to the big house, we sit on a great big sofa; my feet don't go halfway to the floor and it smells fusty. The room is so big, it's always cold. I don't like being there much, it's a bit boring, and I have to be quiet and sit still. But I know we will have a special treat that I always love - beef dripping on bread! Miss Anderson tells me it's the juice that forms under the lard when the joint of beef that they manage to have every week is roasted. She sounds a bit peeved when she sez 'every week'. To me, it's another thing that's scrumptious! It's brought into us on a tray by a lady in a black dress who Miss Anderson calls the Housekeeper. I always wonder which house she keeps.

The very old lady we go to see calls it her house, and a man who can't talk very well lives there also. I think he is a big boy with an old face. I hear Miss Anderson and the old lady talking about him; they say he is not normal. I think he comes from a foreign land because he has a flat face and slanty eyes.

Me and Mo are members in a little gang of three girls and two of the smaller boys. They aren't like the big boys in the other gang, they are kind. In fact, they love to play house and sometimes they like to be the Mam, and us their kids. They even like to put headscarves on and carry an old handbag we have in our den.

Some strange people stay in the cottage on the other side of the road from us. These people are always dressed in long black clothes, strange black hats and the men have long beards and ringlets at the side of their heads. They aren't allowed to leave the village; I don't think they ever go farther than the village shop. They speak a language we don't understand. We all think they are witches so are scared of them. "Let's go to see the witches", one of the big boys sez. What that means is we throw stones at their door and run away when they answer. They always smile at us, sometimes they hold sugar cubes out. We know if they catch us we will never be seen again so we never have the courage to take the sugar. It is very tempting, sweet things are in such short supply. One day Miss Anderson catches me playing at the witches' house with the others. She is really angry with me, marches me home and makes me sit down while she tells me about them. "Listen to me". She is angry! "They are called Jews and they come from Germany. They have had to run away because the other Germans are being horrible and cruel to them and some of their families have been taken away to prison". Now I feel very sorry for them. They still scare me to death, but I don't throw stones any more.

I tell the boys what Miss Anderson has told me. So instead of throwing stones, they march up and down outside of the cottage with their finger under their noses, saluting and saying "Hiel Hitler!". I know that's naughty too so I don't do it, but it makes me laugh. Of course we don't realise how cruel it is. All Germans are the same to us.

Miss Anderson's house doesn't have any upstairs rooms. It is very small and has a lovely garden outside. She has a little terrier dog called Sam and she loves him like he's her baby. I like him a lot too. We go on really long walks with him. The garden has three real tombstones which are only small and all in a row. They are for pets of Miss Anderson that have died. One was a cat, the other two were dogs, all called Sam. Miss Anderson has forget-me-nots growing across them. We pick wild flowers on our walks and put them on the graves as well.

One day we go on one of our picnics to the big field with cows in it. Right in the middle is a little wooden building surrounded by a small barbed-wire fence to keep the cows out. I don't know why the building is here, it's like a one-roomed house. In it are chairs and tables that we can put outside on sunny days. We sit and eat our picnic with the cows crowding round watching us from the other side of the fence. Today, we eat our picnic inside cos it has turned very dull and windy.

Sam keeps barking at the door so Miss Anderson tells him off. "He wants to go home early and I think he's right". We start to pack up our bags and put Sam on his lead. When we open the door, the biggest head I've ever seen pokes nearly through the door, in fact almost into the room. Miss Anderson slams the door shut and pushes a chair under the handle.

"My goodness, we are in trouble". Miss Anderson sounds scared, "That is the angriest bull I have ever seen". I have never seen anything as big in my life, it's bigger than the whole of me, and that's just its head. She sez, "Take Sam to the window". By now Sam is almost barking his head off. I do as I am told, and she puts another chair behind the door as the bull thunders round to the window.

Miss Anderson shushes Sam. I pull him away and she closes the shutters that are inside. We hear the thunder of hooves and I think the bull is going to charge us. Sam starts again. "I'm sure the bull has broken through the fence to get to the cows. Quiet, Sam", Miss Anderson sounds scared. He does finally shut up, thank goodness. It's getting dark very quickly now, and I'm more and more frightened. I can tell Miss Anderson is really scared and worried as well. We can hear the bull outside, snorting and stomping with rage.

"Right Jane, we will have to wait here until the farmer comes. I hope he realises what's happened". Miss Anderson pulls the rug from out of our basket she puts it on a chair and tells me, "Sit on here". I do as I'm told, I'm glad of the rug as I'm feeling quite cold by now. We can't even light the oil lamp we have in the room in case it makes the bull angrier. Miss Anderson looks through the drawers and boxes in the room.

She finds a torch, holds it up and sez, "This will be useful, Jane you have to be a brave girl. Go over to the front window and open the shutters. Watch the window and tell me if the bull moves from the front. You must tell me right away because the bull can move very fast". She sounds so-o-o scared. I just don't want to see it. I can't speak so I nod very hard. I open the shutters and the bull is there! Miss Anderson opens the back window and climbs up onto the flat roof. The bull hears her and goes thundering round, but she is on the roof by now. I close the shutters right away and push the bar across. She starts to flash the torch on and off, for hours and hours. Then the torch goes off and won't go on again.

Miss Anderson shouts, "Go to the front window again dear, take Sam on his lead. Open it a little until you hear the bull moving, let Sam bark. You must close it as soon as you hear him".

When I hear the pounding of the bull's hooves as it charges round I drag Sam away, slam the shutter and put the bar on. This time the bull reaches far enough to hit the door again, but it doesn't give way. Miss Anderson has managed to get back in through the window but she is frozen almost stiff. "All we can do now is wait", she sez quietly. "Sam, lie down and stop barking". He does as he's told. "Don't cry dear, we are going to be quiet as mice then he might go away. It's dark now and he won't know we are here". She closes the other shutters. Miss Anderson lights the lamp and puts it near us. She roots through the cupboards and finds another wool rug, then takes the cushions off the garden chairs. She passes one to me. "Lovely, we have one each for our heads". I'm not sure about putting my head on it as it smells. "It's just a bit of damp dear, so stop complaining". If I was at home I would get shouted at for moaning but Miss Anderson never shouts at me.

"Right", she tells me, "We are here for the night, so let's get ourselves organized". Miss Anderson always likes to be organized. She gets another rag rug and puts it on top of the one on the floor, places the cushions at the top and covers us over with the two wool rugs. It is still cold so she sez, "Well Jane, we'll have to cuddle together and Sam will help".

I have Sam on one side and he is like a hot water bottle. Miss Anderson lies down on the other side but I am not happy, she is skinny and cold.

"I don't want to stay, Miss Anderson", I complain.

"No dear, neither do I, but we have no choice. Just got to make the best of it; think of it as an adventure", she replies.

"It's like being in the shelter, with no bombs". I say to her.

She cuddles me. "Oh my dear, I forget what you children have gone through, I'm sorry". I don't know why she's sorry. She didn't drop the bombs on us.

It's getting light and there's a terrible noise in the field. We get up

69

and look out of the window. It looks like the bull is trying to kill a cow. It's terrible! The bull is on the cow's back and is biting her neck, I get upset cos cows are nice. Miss Anderson sez, "Don't worry, the cow will be OK", but I don't believe her. We hear the sound of a tractor. "Thank goodness". She sounds relieved. The farmer has heard the noise in the field and come to have a look. When she calls out to him, his face is a picture!

"What on earth are you doing here at this time of the morning?" he asks Miss Anderson. She looks like she is going to explode.

"Don't ask! This is your fault. If you had kept your fences in better condition, we wouldn't have been here all night".

He is shocked. "I'll get you out on my tractor. I'm sorry the bull has trampled the fence down, he's so desperate to get to the cows. I've had to keep him in for a while".

I tell him, "I don't think he's friends with the cows, he was standing on one trying to eat it". They think it's funny but I don't.

We are on the tractor and now we can see how lucky we have been. There isn't much fence left. It has been trampled into the ground. The farmer's shocked, and sez, "If the bull had charged the building it would have collapsed like match wood". All I want to do is go home to have my breakfast – I'm starving - and then I want to go to bed. Miss Anderson lets me have the morning off school. Being such a small village, everyone at school has heard about it, and I'm quite famous all afternoon.

Miss Anderson has a lovely doll, dressed in beautiful clothes and a very pretty pot face with eyes that open and close when it wants to go to sleep. It has beautiful long curly hair, a rosebud mouth and pink cheeks. She has it carefully packed away in her blanket box. She'll let me take it out when she's there and I nurse it. I can't play with it properly though. Miss Anderson has kept it since she was a little girl. Sometimes she lets me gently brush its beautiful hair. I've always wished for a doll like it, but it's wartime and no dolls are being made. Well, not for ordinary people like me. One day, Miss Anderson tells me I can have her doll when she dies. I am so excited as she is quite old! I look every morning to see if she has, but I'm never to have the doll.

I keep asking Miss Anderson when she is going to take me to see my big brother Tom. Then out of the blue, one day she sez she's going to take me that very day. She has what she calls 'her old Morris car', and has saved her petrol coupons so that she has two gallons in the tank. She's never used it while I've been here so I thought it must be broken. But it isn't, and we are going to the farm where Tom is. This is something new to me. I haven't been in a car before, only on a bus. Miss tells me it's a few miles to the farm where Tom is. It seems a very long way away. I don't think Miss Anderson is used to the car any more as it's very bumpy and I'm sure I hear her say the swear word 'damn' under her breath. I know about swear words. Mo's big brother told us some and Mam used to tell Dad off for using really bad ones, she used to say he was taking God's name in vain.

When I see my Tom, he looks very different - dead skinny and pale, but I'm so glad to see him! I had thought he was a long, long way from me, but now I know he isn't all that far away, I feel a lot better. The very day we visit, a huge boar gets out of the sty. It is enormous and has big tusks sticking out of the side of its nose. I have never seen anything like it before. Tom tells me it is a male pig and is very, very dangerous. We all have to run into the beck to get away from it. Miss Anderson sez she isn't happy about getting her good brogue shoes wet. The boar grabs a chicken that's running around the yard, it eats it alive. It's so awful I'm sick, and Miss Anderson has her hands over her eyes. The farmers chase it and beat it with big sticks and pitchforks until they get it back into the pen. The farmers are two brothers and a sister, they don't seem very nice.

When we get back to the lodge, Miss Anderson sends for the Vicar. She tells him my Tom is being badly neglected and starved on the farm. They decide Miss Anderson should write to my Mam and tell her. Mam comes almost right away to take him home. "At last", I think, "I will be going too". But I'm still to stay away and what's more I have to move again. When Mam comes to collect Tom from the Vicar, me and Miss Anderson are there to see her. She notices I scratch my head and looks into my hair. I have biddies!

"Are you blind, woman?", Mam shouts at Miss Anderson when she tells her she thought I had heat bumps. "You must be stupid!". Mam is never one to hold back and is really nasty to Miss Anderson. Miss Anderson answers her angrily, "You are a cheeky and ungrateful woman. You should take care of your children yourself". The argument ends up with Mam packing my bags. She then takes me back again to see the Vicar. I'm confused, I am quite happy with Miss Anderson. I haven't even asked to go home. I really want to stay so I can get the doll. The Vicar sends for the village nurse and she washes and cleans my hair. Then she tells Mam she knows of a place where I can go to live. I don't plead with Mam to take me home any more. In fact, I think I am never going home and Mam will just come to see me now and again. She has brought me a parcel. Inside, there is a new dress and knickers, pencils and paper, and a new rag doll that my Nana has made for me. I miss my little Nana so much my tummy hurts. Mam never posts things to me now, because of the people at the farm keeping my parcel for their own little girl.

Mam is horrified when she sees our Tom. He tells her and the Vicar what has been happening to him. It seems the boys had only turned up for school on the first day as it had been such a long way for them to walk they decided not to go again. No one ever checked up to see where they were or if they were all right. The people who run the farm had taken two of the biggest boys off the bus. They were made to take two evacuees, so they took boys they could use as cheap labour.

Mam sez thank goodness our Tom has always been a clever kid and he has quite a lot of common sense. But he's barely survived, even by stealing food. At the farm, the only food they have been fed every day is bread and potatoes. The farm had big flitches of bacon hanging up in the dairy. The farmer's sister used to check that the boys never touched it but Tom got fly to that. He'd climb up and cut it off from the top. He had to collect the eggs for the farmer, so he would take some of the eggs and hide them. He used to cook them on a fire in an old tin. They had shown him how to kill chickens by wringing their necks. He would steal one every so often and let the farmers think a fox had got it. He would scatter some of the feathers and drip some blood around their nests. Then he would roast it over a fire and he would keep the insides to fish with. He'd go to a private river and fish for salmon and eels. He used to get milk from the cow to drink. He tells me he even baked a hedgehog in clay. But he still never has enough to eat, and has got thinner and weaker.

I listen as he tells them what he had to do to eat on the farm. I am almost sick as he gives all the gory details on how he kills and cleans the hens and fish. The other boy evacuated with him used to eat whatever Tom could steal or catch. He was very, very scared of the farmers. If they caught Tom up to anything, he would tell on him. One day one of the men at the farm had caught them stealing apples. The other boy told him that it was Tom's idea and he had made him help him. As a punishment, the farmer threw Tom in with the boar. It was only because Tom was quick thinking that he lived. The boar is a huge wicked creature and could have eaten him, never mind the hen, if it had got to him. He had jumped onto the hayrack, and spent all night there before they let him out. I feel like crying when he tells them about it. The Vicar doesn't seem to believe him. Mam sez she will go back one day and get them for it. But she doesn't! At least he's going home, I wish I was.

CHAPTER NINE
ANOTHER HOME

Mam takes me to see the family that the nurse told her would take me in. I stand in front of the lady.

"Oh what a beautiful child!", she looks at Mam. Mam is not very impressed, she looks at me, "Is she?". Major Eversham speaks in a very posh voice, "Yes she is, come here dear, do you want to live here with us?".

I think this is my chance to say I would rather go home. But Mam shakes her head, "She doesn't get a choice, I can't have her home". Mrs Eversham looks at Mam and asks, "Why not, my dear?". Mam goes all nice and sez, "It's not safe and I'll have my time cut out working and taking care of Tom as he is really very ill". Major Eversham looks at Mrs Eversham. "Well darling what do you think?" She looks at me and sez, in her gentle voice, "I would love to have you to live with us, Jane. What do you think?". I think, I'm not going home and this looks as good a place as any. I nod my head. I want to go with Mam really, but I know I haven't a choice and it won't work if I cry, although it is what I really want to do.

Major Eversham's a tall soldier, with a posh uniform and he looks very handsome - he has brown brylcreamed hair which makes it flat and shiny, and a mustache like David Niven; our Mam likes him! He never seems to have to go away for a long time, like Dad does. I haven't even seen him since he went away, Mam sez he's in the Eighth army.

Major Eversham lets me help him when he works in the garden. He has a gardener, but he looks after the vegetable garden, sez it's his war effort. I like it here. There is always a robin hopping around when he's digging, and sometimes it sits on his shovel. I love to watch it pecking away at the ground then suddenly fly off with a big fat worm hanging from its beak.

Mrs Eversham's mother lives with us as well. She sits in a wicker wheelchair all day; she's very, very old. I can't understand her when she talks to me, but she has a nurse who knows what she's saying. I walk into her bedroom one morning and she's sitting on a chair with no hair on her head. I run away to tell Mrs Eversham. She explains that her mother's hair has fallen out because she's old, that's why she wears the thing she calls a wig. After the first scare, I'm fascinated watching the nurse putting her wig on. She has three, all the same goldy colour, but different styles. They look quite silly because she has a really, really wrinkled face. Sometimes when everyone is downstairs, I sneak into her room and try one on. I don't suit gold hair!

The big house is surrounded by trees but not as many as the house down the drive. In the morning, I wake up before anyone else except for cook. I love to sit on the window seat in my bedroom, listening to the rooks making their raucous cawing noises. They are big, wicked looking birds and in my storybook at school they live with witches. I'd like to be a witch, I love their long black cloaks, skirts and pointy shoes, and they fly about on broomsticks. I am still waiting for my wings to grow so that I can fly. I would be happy to fly on a broomstick for now. Actually, I would like to go to Germany and put spells on all the Gerries, then I really could go home - I'm gone seven now and want to see my friends so much. I suppose I am lucky to be living in such luxury. Each bedroom is a different colour. Mine is the blue room which is my favourite colour so I'm very lucky. Mrs Eversham has the green room and her mother is in the pink one. Major Eversham has his own room but it isn't a pretty colour, it's brown and I think it's dull. My Dad doesn't have his own room which means he'll have to sleep with Mam again when he comes home.

The Evershams are really very kind to me. I have new, pretty dresses and big satin ribbons in my hair. I have a lady who comes in to teach me to speak properly, I haven't to say 'cos', or 'sez,' or shout or scream anymore, and I'm very, very clean. Still, I am never as happy here as I was at Mo's Mam's cottage. I miss the comfort of the nights when the four of us all shared one bed.

There's a great commotion in the garden this morning. Some men have come to take away the big iron gates at the end of the drive. Mrs Eversham is out there, very upset.

"How dare you. You cannot take my beautiful gates". She sounds very posh and bossy.

"We are very sorry Missis, they are needed for the war effort". The man doesn't sound sorry. I wish Major Eversham was here.

"My husband, Major Eversham, has had to go to London to the War Office. Will you wait until I get in touch with him?" she pleads.

"We can't, these gates have to come now", the man scowls.

"What can I do?" Mrs Eversham is really upset now.

"Teck it up wit' War Office", the man smirks.

Mrs Eversham rushes off and I think she's crying.

"Right lads, ger 'em off", the man sez. Then he sez, "This lot with their big houses think they don't have to give anything up. Well, they're wrong".

I go up to him and kick his leg, "I'm not one of this lot and you're a horrible man". I run away quick leaving the other men laughing. It isn't fair because Major and Mrs Eversham do lots for the war effort. That's why they've got to put up with me and they are very kind. In fact, now I would like Major Eversham to be my Dad.

I think the man is after me. As he walks towards me, Mrs Park the cleaner shoves me behind her back, but he just gives her a piece of paper. Then leans towards me, "Tell her she can claim them back at the end of the war". He smirks again, "Come on lads, let's go and upset the next toff". I kick out at him again, but because I'm behind Mrs Park I can't reach and I run off. He laughs. When I'm a safe distance away, I stick my tongue out then spit. I wish our Tom was here. He can spit further than any of his gang.

It looks awful without the gates. I see Mrs Eversham looking out of the window, still crying. I feel sad for her, but in our street everyone gave lots of pans, tin mugs, and anything metal, up. They were pleased to help the war effort. They have to build ships and guns with them.

The big house is the last place I have to stay. Mrs Eversham has no kids of her own and has asked Mam if she can keep me. They tell Mam I would never be short of anything. Mam sez no and I'm glad. I like Mr and Mrs Eversham, but I love Mam and Tom. Now Mrs Eversham has got sick and can no longer look after me. They've sent for Mam and she's come and is taking me home at last.

Our town hasn't been bombed as much since I was evacuated, and as Tom's already at home, Mam has decided that I'll be less trouble back home with them. I go to hug her, "Thank you Mummy, I'm so glad to be going home with you". She looks at me in amazement, pushes me away and sez, "They've turned you into a snotty little snob...'Mummy'! Mam is good enough for me".

CHAPTER TEN
HOME AT LAST

I am home at last and so happy. I go to a bigger girls' school, not the infants' anymore. Mam sez I am a big girl now and I can look after myself more. She lets me carry my candle up to bed in its candle holder. I have to carry it carefully so as not to spill the hot fat. I still like to sleep with Mam when I can but she goes out of a night now, so now I am back sharing with Tom. I would rather sleep in Mam's bed even when she's out, but when I ask if I can, she tells me it would disturb me too much. Sometimes I do get disturbed when I hear music and laughing downstairs. I hear people having such a good time and I would like to go down. When I can fly properly, I'll fly downstairs and Mam won't hear me, then I can see the people who are having such a good time.

We never see Mr Brown, our lodger, of a night. I think he goes to bed very early. Mam leaves me and Tom in our beds and sez not to bother him unless we have any trouble. I don't think he knows he's minding us! Because Tom has to steal his matches, Mr Brown still doesn't like him, so Tom warns me not to tell him about anything. Nothing happens much, except for Tom scaring me with ghost stories. So Mr Brown is never disturbed.

When I moan about Mam going out, she sez, "I have to work all the time and deserve a bit of peace away from you, and it's no-one's business". She does have to work hard and has gone thinner than ever, she only eats dry cream crackers. Good job Dad isn't here, he would tell her off. When she gets ready to go out, she puts gravy browning on her legs and draws a pencil line up the back so it looks like she has stockings on. Her hair is in a roll on her neck and she has a long roll across the top. She makes them by putting her old stockings under her hair and rolling it up. She has a red fox fur which she puts around her neck; she looks like Dorothy Lamour. I don't even like looking at the fox fur, it has legs and everything, poor thing. When I wish she didn't have to go out all the time, she tells me, "Dad's money isn't enough to live on".

After I come home, she got a new job. She drove a horse-and-cart and worked as a milk lady, but has now given it up cos she had a terrible shock. One day after I came home from school, I was playing in the back street when a neighbour comes out to tell me that Mam was going to be late. She tells me, "Your Mam can't come home yet, her horse has been hurt. It's bolted and a shaft off the cart has gone into its body". She sez it has happened about five streets away.

Me and the kids in our gang decide to go to see it, not realizing just how awful it will be. We all go off, as excited as if we are going to the pictures. I feel quite important as it is *my* Mam that the accident has happened to. I wish I had never gone to see it when I see its huge eyes filled with pain. I know then, I will never forget that poor horse. It is shot, and is too much for Mam. She gives up driving the milk cart.

Mam has become a land girl now, working on a farm just outside of the town. It's classed as part-time because Mam has us but she still works five full days a week. She is very slim now and on the farm wears some tight trousers she calls jodhpurs. When I go to a shop with her, a lot of men whistle at her. Some old men shout at her and tell her women shouldn't wear men's pants.

The neighbours keep their eye on all the kids in the street when our Mams aren't there. Apart from the odd air raid, we are safe most of the time. One day when I'm playing out and skipping with the girls, I trip over the rope and snap the strap on my sandal. It's nearly time for Mam to come home and I sit howling on the pavement, I know I'm gonna in trouble. A lad comes out from one of the houses. He's a big lad, almost a man.

"What's up?", he kneels down beside me and I show him my sandal. "Come on", he picks up my sandal and takes me into his house, "I'll sew it back on for you". He gets his Mam's sewing box out. "Come here", he pulls me onto his knee. While he threads the needle, he keeps dropping the cotton on my knee and squeezes my leg, higher and higher every time he picks it up. I start to feel really scared and uncomfortable; I'm not sure why, but I know I want to leave. I hear my Mam shouting my name, she always shouts for me when she comes in. Up until now, whenever I try to get off his knee, he has kept hold of me. Now I say, "There's mi Mam", and he lets me go. I daren't tell Mam about the lad because although I can go into most of our neighbours' houses, she has told me never to go anywhere with a strange man. I am not quite sure why I am so frightened. Nothing really serious has happened.

My Tom is really, really poorly with his throat and is turning red all over which Mam sez it's a rash. The doctor comes and he is rushed into the Isolation Hospital with scarlet fever. He is really very ill and Mam tells me we're not allowed to visit him until he is not contagious. I think that means when he isn't red any more. He's away for over six weeks! When he is a bit better, Mam bunks me up to wave at him over the very high hedge around the hospital. It is good to see he is still there. I always have a fear that when people go away they won't come back.

When Tom comes home from hospital, Mam decides we'll have a photograph taken to send to Dad to show him that Tom is better. I have forgotten what Dad looks like. Mam's not even sure that Dad will get her letters. She tells us, "He is in the middle of the war and his few letters are all chopped up when I finally get them". She also tells us, "He has so little to write about so they're more like letters from a stranger". He is now, to me, just a man in a photo that Mam has on the sideboard.

To have our photo taken, Mam lets me wear a beautiful blue satin dress. She made it for my auntie's wedding when I was a flower girl. She spent ages on smocking it across the bodice. She managed to buy me a straw bonnet which she lined with satin to match my dress. It is the best dress and bonnet I've ever had. The material for the dress, like lots of other things, just appeared but I never knew where from. There is always someone somewhere who can get you what you want, at a price. Even us kids know who the 'Spivs' are. I think if our Tom was older he might be one himself. They are better dressed than anyone else and they all wear suits, slicked down hair and shiny shoes, but it is their ties that really give them away, they are wide with a big knot. Nobody speaks about it though; there are just ways of getting hold of things that aren't in the shops as long as you can find the money. It must be very hard for my Mam, having to work long hours and bring two children up as well, especially with the problems of the war and all the shortages.

Now, one of the things I hate is having to wear boy's shoes because they last longer. I always wanted a pair when I was five but now I'm older I would rather look like a girl, especially when I play out with the boys. Still, I know I'm lucky to have them. My friend Valerie is very shy and she had to stay off school because she had no shoes. Teacher was cross with her when she wouldn't tell her why she had been off and kept her in class after school. When she told her mam why she had been kept in, she was hurt for her. So she went to tell her teacher why Valerie couldn't come to school. But teacher makes it worse for Valerie. She asked all the class to ask their mams if they had a spare pair of shoes for her. She cried because she was so embarrassed.

My shoes are sensible lace-ups, and last longer than girls'. Mam put studs in them as soon as we got them. Now my feet have grown she uses the small shoe shape on the shoe last. This makes my shoes great for sliding in, and the playground at school is the best place to do it. One day I am running and sliding in the schoolyard, having a good time, when I misjudge my slide and hit a wooden trapdoor that's in our playground. I go down hard, hitting the big grey bolt-and-padlock that fastens it...with my head! I remember walking into school, sitting down at my desk, leaning my head on my slate and seeing Teacher. She went to bring a bucket when I told her I was feeling sick. I throw up before she comes back, then I remember nothing until I wake up and feel Teacher's hand on mine. She is sitting beside me. I am very sick again and a strange lady is seeing to me. I know it is a strange person by her voice but when I open my eyes I can't see anyone. I cry for Teacher and tell her I can't see. She squeezes my hand and sez, "Don't worry Jane, you're in an ambulance, you'll soon be OK". The other lady sez, "Can you see me now?". I cry, "No". She sez, "Are you sure?". I cry again, "I can't", and then am sick all over her.

I don't remember anything else until I wake up in a hospital bed a few days later. I have the most horrible headache, and there is what seems like a thousand babies screaming their heads off in the small room. It turns out there are only two. My poor head has made it feel like a crowd. I have given myself a really bad concussion. I have to stay in hospital another week. I quite enjoy it as I get treats that I don't usually get. Teacher sends me a book and a pencil, and an apple. But I don't get the apple! Mam lets Tom eat it on the way to see me. He tells me as soon as he comes in and Mam clips his ear for telling me. The hospital is a big old building. It seems to be all huge high corridors with cracked ceilings and cracked shiny cream painted walls; the blitz has caused some of the cracks.

They take me out of the small room when I'm a bit better. I'm put into a ward with other kids and some grown-up ladies. The beds are iron frames and not very comfortable, with a rubber sheet under the cotton sheet in case we wee our bed; they make you sweat. They also rattle and make creaking sounds all the time and keep us awake of a night. Some of the ladies pump a lot, snore loudly and grunt as well.

Every morning when the nurses make our bed, the white sheet is turned back and tucked in tight across our chest with our arms sticking out. We have to lay very quiet and stiffly without moving. We aren't allowed out of our beds in case we make them untidy before Matron comes around. Matron is a scary sight. Everyone jumps to attention when she's around. I think even the doctors are afraid of her. I know she scares the living daylights out of me. She always reminds me of a ship as she billows through the wards, she doesn't seem to walk. I think she is floating on air. Perhaps she has wings; I think I am finally growing mine, I can see two lumps sticking out of my back now I can see in the mirror. Mam sez they are my shoulder-blades and it's time to grow up. I don't believe her as she is a grown-up and doesn't believe in angels or fairies! Matron is the cleanest person I've ever seen in my life, a big lady and glows with cleanliness. She wears a blue dress with a huge pure white pinny over it. Her white hat shaped like a triangle is so stiff it looks like she has wings coming out of the sides. She passes us by and never ever smiles. We can hear her rustling from wards away. The hospital is run by her and she is law. There isn't a kid here who would make a mess of their beds once they have met her.

CHAPTER ELEVEN
OUR GANG

Although it is still wartime, it's early summer and seems to be sunny and bright all the time. My very best friend is called Alice. We play out for hours in our back street.

"Come on Jane", Alice sez, "Let's go and get the kids off Mrs Welsh and take them to the park".

The Welshes are a big family! Mrs Welsh has a new baby every year, so she always has a baby to take out. The pram is an old battered thing with a buckled wheel, just a bit of blanket in the bottom and a very nasty pillow at the top. Still, we don't care about things like that. By the time we're going to the park there's always quite a group of us. There are always three or four little Welshes. We shove the smallest baby up the top of the pram and stick one or two of the smallest toddlers in at the bottom. We are never intentionally cruel to them, but it must be hard on them. We love them in our own childish way. One day in the park, all of us kids are running down the big grassy hill pushing the old pram. It hits an extra hard bump and topples over. There are babies and kids flying about all over the place. I think God has taken care of us because apart from a few skinned knees and grass stains we are all OK.

Another day we decide to go to the park, quite a large collection of motley kids. This time the youngest Welsh baby is dirtier than usual, so first we take it to my house to wash it because Mam's out. We can't get its vest off so we sit it in the kitchen bowl and wash it with its vest on, it gets very wet. I tell Alice it could catch pneumonia. "'Course it won't, it'll soon dry in the sun". She's ten now and I'm not, so she must be right. I do hope she's right because it isn't used to having its face washed, never mind its little body. We take those kids with us every time we go to the park all that summer and they are fine, skinny but healthy.

We don't have the little ones today, so we go up the Abbey. We can't push the old pram that far. We have a good time in the Amphitheatre, good job we didn't have the little kids in the pram up that hill! When we go down by the river, we have a sad time, and find a dead sheep just lying there in the grass. We all crowd round poking it to make sure it's dead. I think we should say a prayer, but Rose has a better idea. She sez, "Should we bury it?". We all think that's a great idea.

It's a lot heavier than we thought and it *really* stinks. When we start to drag it to some bushes, lots of bluebottles fly off it. Then it dawns on us we haven't anything to dig a hole with. We all sit round it to think. Barry sez, "Let's cover it with sticks and stuff", so we spend a very happy hour finding lots to cover it up. Someone even found a piece of old sacking to wrap it up and we make it a cross out of twigs. Rose sez, "God Bless this sheep". We decide it should have a name because God won't know which one it is. Now everyone wants to name it. Barry sez, "I'm gonna call it Doris after mi Mam, and I'm the oldest". So, Doris it is. When we've finished we sit down to eat our bread and jam and share a bottle of tap water, feeling really happy. When I tell Mam how kind we were, she plays pop.

"It's a wonder you all don't get diphtheria, it must have been full of maggots. Go and wash your hands right now". I can't see it being any good washing now but I do as I'm told.

I still have my birthday swing on my back gate. I come home from school and sit, swinging in the sun, singing and talking to myself. These times as I fly up high, I can't wait for my wings to grow. These are happy uncomplicated days.

Sometimes, things still go wrong though. Dad's allotment is quite a long way from where we live. Mam keeps it going so we can have vegetables. There's a shed on it where she hides Dad's bike so it will be here for him when he comes home. But one day, she comes home very upset - the hut has been broken into and Dad's bike has been stolen. The neighbour next door saw who took it. It was my Grandad! Grandad has stolen it to sell cos he is in trouble again with gambling debts. Mam sez he is always in trouble because he is a really heavy gambler. She shouts and screams at him but he tells her he had to do it or he will be beaten up. He's already taken my Nana's diamond jewellery and sold it. She was quite well off when she was younger, until she met Grandad. Grandad has taken it all and she never complains.

Our allotment is a lovely place. I sit in the sun for hours. Listening to all the birds singing, watch the brightly coloured butterflies stretching their wings in the warmth of the sun and lazily listen to the busy bumblebees buzzing in and out the flowers. I nibble sour crabapples off our neighbour's trees but they are so sour I have to have a quick drink out of the hosepipe. The neighbours tell our Mam she can make jam with them, but they would take all of our sugar ration. When we are here, Mam gardening and me helping, we forget all about the whistling bombs, incendiaries, dead people and being so scared. But even this comfortable place has to change. A Gerrie bomber drops its last bomb right into the middle of it. All that is left is a great big hole called a 'crater', and not a single thing is left of our allotment to ever say it has been there. Mam and me stare into the hole. Then she starts to laugh, although she is crying as well. I laugh with her but don't know what for. The weird thing is that the bomb has dropped into the only place no-one lives at, but our allotment is surrounded by houses and a lot of them are badly damaged with lots of walls cracked, ceilings down and broken windows.

The gangs of kids in our street all know that if we see a queue, we have to send half of us to stand in the line. The other half run home fast to get an adult to take our place. We know whatever is on sale, we want it, and if we don't need it, we can swap it for something else. We are lucky because my Nana had a little grocer's shop before the war started. When she heard war declared on the wireless, she closed it and took all the tinned and dried goods off the shelves. She shares it with us and it means we have more food for a bit longer than other people. She gave us a double biscuit tin full of rice.

It is good because we can have rice pudding and cold, sliced rice pudding cake (which is rice baked very thick and sliced cold). We enjoy it but what spoils it a bit is that it has no butter and very little sugar in it now. Sometimes Mam puts some homemade bramble jelly on it or a few raisins in it when it is cooking. I don't like raisins; sometimes Mam boils them with barley then pours the water off and makes me drink it, sez it's good for my kidneys.

If we have visitors, Mam gives them a slice of the rice pudding cake with a cup of tea, and they really enjoy it. Tom and me share the skin off the top of the pudding; we call it Grandad's toffee. When I go to my Nana's, I stand by my Grandad when he has his tea, especially if he has an egg. He always dips a piece of bread in his egg for me to have some of his yolk; it tastes so good.

My aunty Mona lives at home with my Nana and Grandad. Mam sez she's very smart and has lots of boyfriends. She has a sailor friend and he gave her a bunch of bananas, so she gives us one each. I'm so proud of mine I take it to school to show everyone. I've no idea what it tastes like but it smells lovely. I show it to everyone in the playground. Teacher comes out and looks at it and sez, "It's bad, you can't eat it. Come with me". She takes me to the wastebasket and makes me throw it away. I have probably mauled it to death, but I was really looking forward to eating it. I go back to the basket when school finishes but it's not in there.

We have American soldiers in town. I think they are here as we are a shipyard town. Aunty Mona goes out with one of them; he's nice and gives her all kinds of things: chewing gum, chocolate and stockings. She gives me some of the chocolate and Tom some gum. Aunty Mona and Buchwald (that's his name) brought a couple of his friends to Nana's house for tea. This is the first time I see a black man, I can't take my eyes off him.

Aunty Mona tells me, "You are so rude, stop staring".

I'm a bit scared of him, and when he smiles at me his teeth gleam. He smiles at me and sez, "Don't be shy".

I can't stop staring! He asks me if I want to ask him something. So I do, "Will the black rub off if I touch you?"

Aunty Mona sez, "Jane!"

He laughs and puts my hand to his cheek. "Go on, touch my face". It feels like real skin!

I ask, "How did you turn black?"

He tells me, "I'm American but from an African race, and they are black". I don't believe him, but he's nice.

Tom comes home one day and he has an awful bruise on his face. He tells Mam he fell over, then rushes out to the lav. I hear him being really sick so go out to see if he's alright. I was going to get Mam but he tells me not to so I don't. He sez he will tell me why he's sick later. When he comes to bed, he tells me how he got the nasty bruise and why he was so sick. He sez a sailor gave him a bunch of bananas.

"Where have you put them, and can I have one?", I wheedle. He tells me, "I've eaten all of them because if I brought them home, Mam would have wanted to know where I'd got them from". Then he sez, "I went down the docks". "Ah-h, Mam tells you not to go there, you're banned". I know he does a lot of things Mam doesn't like but this is serious. He would really get a slapping for going there and although we fall out a lot, I wouldn't like that. Then he tells me that before he could eat them, he had headed for a spot in a bombed-out house which is the 'den' of his gang. When he got there, a bigger boy from another gang was lying in wait for any of the gang he could get. He attacked Tom and took his bananas. Tom sez he wasn't big enough to stop him, so he followed him with a plank and when he wasn't looking, he knocked him unconscious. I tell him, "Tom, you could have made him die!" Tom sez, "He took my bananas and I knew if I hadn't knocked him unconscious, I wouldn't have got them back and would have had another belting into the bargain". I'm afraid that we are learning that even kids have to be tough to protect themselves.

The older he gets, the less I see of Tom. He's always out and, according to Mam, up to no good. I hear Mam talking to Mrs Carr, "Tom isn't a bad boy but he's naughty and strong-willed. It's probably just as well that he is, or he would never have survived when he was evacuated to that stinking farm". She still gets really mad and upset when she thinks about it.

Tom comes home one day with a great big bloody bruise on the back of his knee. Mam bathes it and asks him how he got it. He moans and expects sympathy. Tells Mam, "A man on the market kicked me". Mam gives him a clip round the ear and shouts, "You must have done something, he wouldn't do it for now't, serves you bloody right". She loves Tom very much, but I know he worries her to death at times. Good job she doesn't know half he gets up to.

Today is very sad. Mrs Carr has rushed in all upset to talk to Mam. "Can't talk in front of Jane", she nods at me.

"Must be bad". Mam tells me to go upstairs.

"Arw-- Mam".

"Now", she bawls.

I stamp upstairs because I'm mad. I love to listen to them gossip. I wait and as soon as I hear cups rattling, I carefully creep down to the third step from the bottom, missing the sixth step that squeaks. I know Mam and Mrs Carr won't start talking until they sit at the table with their cuppas.

When Mrs Carr starts talking, she sounds like she's going to cry, "It's terrible, awful; three healthy boys, all dead".

Mam sez, "Who? How?". It's very quiet. I wait.

Then Mrs Carr tells her, "The three lads from two streets away, where the bombs dropped".

"But no bombs have dropped". Mam sounds confused.

"No not now, but when they did. They live on the side that didn't get so badly blitzed".

Mam sez, "What are you going on about? Start at the beginning".

Mrs Carr starts to explain, "They've been poisoned".

Mam gasps, "What?"

Mrs Carr tells her, "Someone said they went to Sowerby Woods for the day and got hungry. They dug up some roots up that looked like potatoes so roasted them over a fire and ate them; they were poisonous! Someone else sez that they found some stuff growing that looked just like rhubarb, and they chewed on it. We won't know till they have an enquiry".

I hear Mam moan; "Oh God, those poor boys, their poor mother".

Mrs Carr sez, "Aye lass".

Mam asks, "Are they having a collection? I think it should be round all the streets, instead of just theirs".

Mrs Carr sez, "Probably someone will, everyone knows the family's very poor. Still, they won't get enough money to give much of a send-off. God love them, they haven't had much in this life. Still, they are going to a better place".

Mam sez, "I hope there is a better place".

Mrs Carr fusses, "Don't say that, of course there is, there has to be".

I am lucky, because our lodger still likes me. He gives me two or three sweets a week out of his rations which makes me like him too. It's a shame that he doesn't like our Tom. Still, I don't tell him I get them. It's Mam's fault really because she still tells Tom to steal matches out of his drawer. Mam knows he counts them, it really upsets him. Now I'm bigger I know Mr Brown is an engineer in the shipyard, so is exempt from going into the forces. When we had to go into the air raid shelter a lot, he was always scared. I could hear his teeth chattering and he shook so much when Mam gave him a mug of tea that it splashed all over the place. I don't think he would be much use in the army. He is very skinny, I never see him eat anything much. He creeps around our house like a ghost.

We are lucky as our air raid shelter stays up. One of my friends' shelters collapsed onto her, her Mam and brothers, and they were badly hurt. Down the bottom of our street, some of the shelters flood when it rains which is very uncomfortable. We are halfway up the hill so are lucky. Now we mainly play in the shelters because the Gerries don't come as often.

CHAPTER TWELVE
HAPPY DAYS

It is a happy time for us kids, everyone takes care of each other. We go to the park often of an afternoon and have picnics. Usually bread with a bit of jam scraped on and a bottle of water. If we are lucky, we have some of that orange juice our Mams gets off the government for us. It tastes horrid but I'm getting used to it, it's better than nothing! I love the malt and cod liver oil that Mam gets for me and our Tom. He doesn't like it but Mam makes him take it because he is run down. Our picnics are happy, if one of the kids doesn't have anything, we share what we've got. When one of us is lucky enough to have an apple, we give each friend a bite and our best friend the stump to finish off. It is quite a job doing it, everyone has to watch that a greedy one doesn't take too big of a bite and there is always a bit of shoving and pushing going on. If I have my boiled sweets off Mr Brown, we all have a suck and no-one is allowed to suck too long. I'm lucky, cos the owner of the sweet is always the one to finish it off. These times are the most happiest times of my life.

One day, one of the big kids out of another gang tells us there is a flasher in the park. He's a man who turns up when all the kids are there. We know he is a bad man cos the big kids say he shows his 'thingy'. None of us girls know what his 'thingy' is *or* what it looks like, but we know he is naughty to do it. If he's there, we go to the top of a hill in the park then shout and jeer at him. We never go too near to him, so don't ever find out what he was really up to. Well! That is, not until the big kids tell us he shows his willy. Ugh, we decide not to go near him again.

Our gang decide to go up to where the paper mills are but I know I'm not supposed to go that far. But there are old railway lines that fill with water, and lots of newts and frogs live around the water so it's fun. Also, there is a lot of sand that the boys dig holes in to crawl into. It is warm so I take off my shoes and paddle in the water, it's a bit green and slimy but it feels lovely. I slip on one of the railway lines and my foot really hurts. When I look down the water has gone all red. I scream my head off and all the kids come to look; a lady with a dog comes over and tells me, "you need to get a stitch in that". I scream louder at that, so she sits me down and wraps her hanky around my foot, then tells my friends to take me home. Luckily my Grandma and Grandad live near the paper mills so I go there. She washes my foot and puts a bandage on it, and it doesn't hurt so much. Grandma sez, "I think you will have to go to hospital, you might need stitches". I think, "no I won't". She gives us a biscuit each and tells me to go straight home. I set off with my friends and feel quite important. The kids let me lean on them as I hop home. Of course, I'd forgotten I would be in trouble for going there.

Mam shouts at me, "You know you shouldn't have gone there - it's dangerous, this is God's way of punishing you". I think, "why me?". I wasn't the only one who shouldn't have gone there. Mam doesn't mention taking me to hospital so that's a relief. Tom tells Mam that once, two boys from his school had died there because the sand hole collapsed on them and they had suffocated. That made her mad at me again, "See", she sez "You could have come home dead, then you would have been in trouble". I couldn't work that out so I thought I'd better be quiet.

We kids never feel deprived. We don't miss a lot of things cos we don't know about them. Life is harder for some; they seem much poorer than other families are. We are all in similar circumstances, but some parents manage better than others and some have a lot more children.

Our houses consist of a front room called a parlour, a kitchen and a scullery downstairs, and three bedrooms upstairs. The back bedroom is always really damp, and lots of the roofs have cracked and broken tiles where they have been damaged through the bombing. Some are so bad that they have holes in. One of my friends from school sez they have to throw cinders out of the fireplace at the pigeons when they come in through the hole, because they make such a noise and wake them up. The smaller kids often sleep in the back bedroom and nearly always have a really bad bronchial cough and green snotty noses all winter. There can be a couple of babies in their Mam and Dad's room, and the big ones sleep in the front. We are lucky as there are only two of us kids in our house. We aren't allowed to sleep in the back bedroom so Tom and me have to share the front bedroom, which he hates.

Most of the boys in our street and at school have what they call pudding basin haircuts. Their hair is usually cut at home, and a lot of the time a pudding basin really is put on their heads so that the line can be as straight as possible. They then have their necks shaved up to the line. Sometimes they have their hair slicked down, flat to their head with brylcream, and they don't just have their faces washed - even the tidemark round their necks has been washed away. You know then they are either going to church, in trouble with school, or have an appointment with the police or court. Sometimes all the boys in one family have their heads completely shaved, and the girls all have pudding basin haircuts. We know why - it's because Nitty Norah has struck again. None of us kids like her. She lines us up then flicks roughly through our hair. I think Mam knows when she's coming because we have our hair washed with Durbac soap the night before and it isn't even bath night. It really smarts and burns our scalps, and stinks to high heaven. Mam rakes through it with the nit comb, our heads hung over an old paper and if we are lucky, nothing drops out.

The better kept boys in our street all wear the same clothes, generally a shirt, a pair of knee-length black or grey trousers, knee-length socks (which usually fall down round their ankles), and sturdy shoes. They are the lucky ones. The rest of the boys have trousers of all lengths and if *they're* lucky, they're patched up; if not so lucky, they have their backsides hanging out, no socks, with shoes of all sizes. Some are so poor they wear wellies for school even in the summer. These poor kids always have a nasty red ring round their legs especially if they wee themselves as so many kids do in these wartime days. I still have accidents.

The better off girls wear little cotton dresses, short socks and sturdy shoes. They are the ones who are better cared for, or have less kids in the family. The others are dressed in anything their Mam can get for them: dresses down to their ankles, shoes with a bit of cardboard or lino in to cover the holes in the soles and often, not even a pair of knickers. It doesn't make any difference to their standing in the pecking order though, the older kids are the boss and you go along with them. Having no socks is no social embarrassment.

There is one thing that I know would make me go up in the world though, and that is a pair of long, thick, brown lisle stockings. My friend Doreen wears a pair of those stockings, held up with elastic garters. I would give up anything that is precious to me, if only Mam would have let me wear them.

Doreen has lots of boyfriends. She goes down the backstreet with them and they kiss her. She has thick, wire-framed glasses and fuzzy hair so I'm sure it's because of those stockings. I plead daily with Mam but to no avail, she is adamant I can't have them. She doesn't realise how much she is stopping me getting a boyfriend. I find out later it's because Doreen takes them down the backstreet and shows them her knickers. I only find that out when one of the boys asks me to show him mine. I daren't do that, Mam might find out. I still hanker after those stockings though, they seem like glamour to me.

Mam has got a better job now working for an insurance firm. It was my Aunty Nellie's job (my Mam's sister). Aunty Nellie is her middle sister and her husband is called Uncle Stanley. I don't like him cos he's always shouting at my Aunty. He is the meanest man you can meet. Mam sez he can peel an orange in his pocket so as not to give anyone a bit. I always wonder if he doesn't get all sticky doing it. He's the only person I know who has a car, but he never lets us in it. Our Tom found some petrol coupons which Mam tells us are like getting gold; ordinary people with cars are only allowed one gallon a week. Mam tells Tom to give them to Uncle Stanley, which he does and he doesn't even say thank you.

I think they are dead posh. They live in a house with a back garden and they have fold-up chairs I can sit on called deckchairs. I'm messing around on one of them one day and it folds up with me inside. Getting out, I tear it and daren't tell Uncle Stanley, so I put it back up and put their Scottie dog in it and make him sit there. Luckily, it is a well behaved dog and does as it's told. I go in and ask my Uncle to come to see how clever his Scottie is. Of course it's torn when we go out, so poor Scottie gets the blame. It's OK though because the dog is the one thing that Uncle Stanley seems to like. Aunty Nellie is really ill and very fragile. She has no children so she likes me staying with her which I enjoy while Mam is working. The only thing I don't like is a thing called 'junket' that's made with a pink powder. It sets like a jelly with water round it. It's horrible but Aunty Nellie sez it is good for me and she makes me eat it. Mam is doing her job cos she had to give it up because of her illness. Uncle Stanley is also an insurance man and was Aunty Nellie's boss. He made my Aunty Nellie go out collecting her money no matter how bad the weather was. My Mam sez that's why she got TB, she used to get really cold and wet but he didn't care.

One day when Uncle Stanley was out, Mam was upset at how ill Aunty Nellie is. He had gone out and left her so Mam called the doctor. At teatime that night, Uncle Stanley comes to our house. He stands in the doorway of our kitchen shouting very loud at my Mam for sending for the doctor, telling her it was none of her business. When he finished shouting, he tells Mam Aunty Nellie has been rushed into hospital with pneumonia. She comes back home for a while. I go to stay with her to keep her company. I dislike Uncle Stanley even more. Although I am young I can tell he often upsets her. When I'm there, she gives Scottie a drink of tea out of her cup. Uncle Stanley jumps up and snatches it away screaming at her, does she want to give the dog what she has.

I know he has said something horrible to her the way she cries. It isn't long before Aunty Nellie goes back into the hospital. It's a special hospital called Meathop Sanitarium in the country. Because there is a lot of TB now, they try to cure it with fresh air and better food. Mam tells us the ward that she's in is open all down one side as they must have fresh air all the time. It works for some but seemingly not Aunty Nellie as I never see her again. Mam cries a lot and tells Mrs Carr who comes in to see her that Auntie Nellie only weighs three and a half stone, and can't speak any more. To show Mam how thin she was she had lifted the blankets and pointed to her legs, Mam really sobs and I cry too. Mrs Carr cuddles Mam. As I listen to them talking, Mam tells her. "It's not fair, she is only twenty six".

The day she is buried, my Mam is really upset again because Uncle Stanley walks out of the church and sez he has to go back to work. Mrs Carr brings me back in from her house where she has been minding me, when Mam comes home. Then Mam tells her what she has found out. "That rotten sod can burn in hell. He's gone to a woman he's been practically living with. She's had a son to him while Nellie was dying. I know that's where he went after the funeral, I'll never forgive him". Mam sobs and sobs, Mrs Platt can't stop her, I cry again. I never see him again. Mam sez he moved this other woman into my Aunty Nellie's home and we move him out of our lives. I decide I am going to drop a great big rock on him when I can fly.

I miss staying with my Aunty Nellie. Now it's back to coming in from school and waiting for Mam to come home when she finishes work. I can go into our house as Mam always leaves the back door open. If I need anything, the neighbours always help. I often have a friend in when Mam's at work. Sometimes I land up in trouble because of showing off and Mam tells me I'm too nosy.

"Let's go upstairs Jane". Doreen knows I'm not supposed to.

"Daren't, Mam sez I haven't to".

"Come on, she won't know". I look at the time.

"OK, I'll show you her fox". I feel important because her Mam hasn't got one.

She scoffs at me, "A fox? Don't believe yer".

We push and shove each other up the stairs, and it feels like an adventure.

"Come and look in Mam's wardrobe, you'll see I'm not a liar". I open the wardrobe door and grab Mam's fox fur, shoving it in Doreen's face.

She shoves it away, "Pooh it stinks, let's have a look. It's dead!"

"Course its dead, silly. Mam wears it round her neck. All the film stars have one". I don't like it myself, but I want her to think Mam's posh.

"Let's look in the wardrobe drawer", Doreen pulls it open.

"What do you want to look in there for?".

91

"My Dad keeps books in theirs that I'm not allowed to read", she replies.

"What kind of books?". I'm fascinated.

"Don't know, never got chance to read them but I think they're rude, your Mam might have some". I root through the drawer but there aren't any. I find something I haven't ever seen before though.

"Look at these, Doreen". They are white things with loops on each end. I put a loop on each of my ears. "I think they are mouth bandages", I say. I look into the wardrobe mirror as I show Doreen.

She scoffs at me. "Stupid, they're what wimen have if they're having a baby". I can't understand how it could make you have a baby but Doreen is a year older than me so must be right. I tingle with excitement!

"Mam's having a baby?", I can't wait to tell everyone. Then I realise I daren't as I shouldn't have been rooting in her bedroom in the first place.

As soon as we go out to play, Doreen tells all our gang. The next day when Mam comes home from work, Mrs Carr knocks at the door and walks in looking mad.

Mam sez, "Hya, Mrs Carr, what's the matter?".

Mrs Carr looks at me funny, then sez to Mam, "Is there something you have to say to me?".

Mam looks at her, "No, I don't think so".

"Well I've something to say to you". Mrs Carr is cross!

"Go on then, say it". Mam looks confused, and shocked at the way her friend is talking to her.

"How could you be such a fool?, Mrs Carr sounds very mad at her. "You didn't have to get pregnant. What are you going to do?".

Mam goes all fainty and sits down, I think it's because she is having a baby. "What the hell are you talking about?".

Mrs Carr looks at me, points and sez, "Ask Jane. She was out in the street telling everyone you are having a baby".

Mam grabs my arm and shakes me, "What have you said that for?". This is me in trouble again and if it gets me out of trouble, I don't mind telling on my friend.

"Not me, Doreen sez you are". I think I'm still in for a slapping for going upstairs. "We saw your baby thing". I whimper for sympathy.

"My baby thing…what are you talking about?"

"Upstairs, in your drawer". Mam looks at Mrs Carr.

Mrs Carr takes my arm, "Right, young lady, let's go to see what you mean". We all go up to Mam's bedroom. I open the drawer and show them the baby thing. Now I'm for it! Instead Mam and Mrs Carr go into the maddest laughter, Mam rolls on the bed and Mrs Carr has tears running down her large face making all her chins wobble.

"Who told you they are for having babies?", Mam asks me.

"Doreen", I repeat, glad to blame her.

"She's wrong. Just wait till I tell her Mam". I don't care, I'm not going to get a slap, and now I know more than her cos she's wrong about them being for babies.

"What are they for Mam?" I ask. Mrs Carr sez, "Mind your own business, lass".

Mam tells me, "You'll know soon enough".

I haven't noticed time passing. I'm gone eight now and there are no more bombs. Life is a lot quieter and although it is as normal as it can be, we are still at war. We have less and less food in the shops and our Mams have a terrible time trying to feed us. It is much worse for some people. One day Mam brings a lot of beetroot home that a gardener has given her. She boils it and I love it, I eat loads of it because it is sweet.

Two days later, Mam goes for a wee after me and I haven't pulled the chain. She rushes in and puts my coat on, then takes me to see Doctor McGill. She tells him I am weeing blood. He sends me over the road to the hospital and I have to wee in a jug! It turns out that I have eaten so much beetroot my wee has turned red. Mam is mad with me for frightening her.

Now it is my turn instead of our Tom to upset her again. I've run across the road at the bottom of the street without looking properly and our big fat paper man has knocked me down with his bike. I just jump up and run away so that he can't tell Mam. The only thing that really hurts is my ankle. I wash the blood off before she gets home and don't tell her. Then I go to bed early because my foot has started to really hurt and it gets much worse in the night. In the morning I can't walk, and have to tell Mam. It has swollen up like a red ball. Mam has to borrow a trolley off a neighbour to push me up to the hospital. I feel daft in a little kid's trolley. They say it is very septic and I have to have things pushed into it. They make me scream. The doctor cleans it up and tells Mam I have to come back the next day to have it lanced. When we get home, after tea, Mam decides I should have it poulticed. She brings in a bowl and fills it with boiling water out of the kettle. Then she puts a clean rag into it without putting cold water in and slaps it onto my ankle. She does this several times. I scream and scream loud enough to bring the neighbours rushing in.

By morning the lump has burst and all the septic oozes out. It leaves a big hole so I still have to go to the hospital to have it cleaned out for a few days. They say I don't have to have it lanced now. I ask Mam what lanced means. She tells me they were going to cut it with a knife. I'm glad they don't have to as I wouldn't be able to walk with just one ankle. When I go back to school, Teacher makes me come out to the front. I think she is sorry for me. Instead she warns all the other kids about crossing the road without looking.

Even in hard times, we kids manage to have fun. Some more than others! Tom is in trouble. He was sat on St George's church roof one day and a policeman saw him. He refused to come down when the policeman asked him to, and after a while the policeman left. Tom thought he had got away with it, so he climbed up again the next day. The policeman saw him again and warned him to get down. Tom wouldn't and sat the policeman out again. He thought he had got away with it again, but this time he hadn't. Tom has been cocky, giving him cheek and not coming down when asked. The bobby hid round the corner and waited to catch him. He took Tom to the police station and kept him there.

I'm sitting on the step when a hu-uge policeman comes to see Mam. He's holding our Tom by the collar of his shirt. Mam isn't happy. She sez Tom's running wild and she clips him round the ear. She is especially mad with him when the policeman tells her they are taking him to court. The next Saturday morning, Tom and Mam have to go to court and she has to pay a fine of one pound, ten shillings. She is very upset.

My Dad's wage with the Army is only about that amount each week and she's had to take a morning off work as well. The same Saturday, in the afternoon, the policeman was at our door again. This time our Tom's been climbing on a bombsite where the Trevellian Hotel was. Part of the building has collapsed on him and he has been rushed to the hospital. He has a fractured skull, leg and other injuries to his body. He is very sick and me and Mam are really worried for a while. Then he gets better and is much more like his usual self. He is able to get out of bed and he'd climbed onto one of the hospital ward's big window seats and slipped down between the window and the seat and has to be rescued. I don't think he's scared of Matron! A nurse tells Mam they are glad he is better so that they could be rid of him. His Teacher sends him an apple, pencils and a book to write in. When we go to see him, I don't eat his apple. Actually I want to, but Mam won't let me. Still he tells me that I can have his pencils and book, he hates writing. He isn't twelve yet and I think my Mam thinks she isn't going to see him grow up. It must be very hard for her.

WWII Ration Books

CHAPTER THIRTEEN
THE FLICKS

We still have seven or eight picture houses in the town. Luckily, they are all open now the bombing has stopped. 'The Flicks' is what we call them, they are the main relaxation for almost everyone in our town. My favourite is 'The Electric' (or 'The 'Lec' as it is known by the local kids). Except I also love 'The Ritz', which we go to on a Saturday morning. It is much posher than The 'Lec and has no fleas.

The Electric Theatre, aka the 'Flea Pit'

A beautiful huge organ comes slowly up from underneath the stage. It's magic! A man sits on a piano stool playing it as it slowly rises up through the stage, all lit up in lovely colours. Then we all sing along to him playing "*Run, Rabbit, Run*", "*Roll out the Barrel*", and many other songs. There is a screen with the words on and a ball bounces on every word so we can follow them, but we don't need it - we know the words by heart and they cheer us up. Everyone cheers and claps when he finishes and very slowly sinks back down into the floor.

Also there is a man who has to keep the boys from being too rowdy. He doesn't do too good a job as he can't talk very well and the boys are rude to him.

He's called Jimmy and they call him 'Jimmy Niff Naff'. I feel sorry for him but he doesn't seem to mind. I am only allowed to go with my Tom, Mam makes him take me and he hates it. What my trusting Mam doesn't realise is that as soon as we are out of sight, he makes me walk on the other side of the road. He does keep his eye on me sometimes but usually he forgets I'm there. It doesn't bother me. I usually try to stop at the Blacksmiths on the way to The 'Lec and watch him shoeing a huge carthorse.

The Blacksmith is always busy, with a scorching fire going in his brazier. He has a couple of long iron things glowing red in it. He wears a big leather apron and looks shiny with sweat which drips off his red face. There's always an audience of us kids as we stand, fascinated, at the door, watching. He sits on a tree trunk, lifts up the huge leg of the horse in front of him, pulls off its old horseshoe with big pinchers, and digs into its hoof with a knife to clean it out. He pulls the red hot glowing horseshoe out of the fire and quickly puts it on the horse's hoof. Then he takes it off and puts it onto another huge tree stump and hammers it into shape. Then quickly plunges it into a water-butt, at which point the whole place is full of steam with a great sizzling noise. It reminds me of the picture of Hell from my religious instruction book at school. He again lifts up the huge leg and taps the shoe onto the horse's hoof. All this happens very quickly and the large horse stands quietly accepting it, so it mustn't hurt it.

After the excitement there, we all rush off totally happy. I have to meet Tom at door of the pictures then he pays me in. Just one of his mates pays to go in! They take turns, he goes off with his other mates and they sneak through the emergency doors, which the boy on the inside opens very carefully. The front seats are forms and when the usherette shows us to the seats, the big boys push that hard to get on together, the smaller ones fall off the other end. They have to find somewhere else to sit, but sometimes we get them back because the big boys get thrown out for being noisy. That is if the man in charge catches them quickly enough, he has a Shepherd's crook which he uses to put round their neck to drag them out.

I go off to find my own younger friends which suits me as there is always a big crowd of us. I have to wait at the door for him when the pictures have finished. The 'Lec picture house is all on one level and it is a penny at the front and tuppence at the back, that's the best end. The last row has double seats on the back row. We sneak up there to see the courting couples if we are bored with the film. Not much goes on and if it does, we don't know what they get up to. If you are caught you can get thrown out. I shouldn't say 'we' really, cos I'm such a wimp I always make sure I am at the back of the gang; that way I'm able to get back to my seat quickly. The 'Lec also has another name, it's called the 'Fleapit'. You can be pretty sure if you haven't a flea going in, you have one when you come out. They have woman going round with a flea spray as you leave, which stinks! Still, we aren't fussy. There is a small picture on before the main film and then the Pathe News which is mainly for grown-ups, although I do like to listen to the huge cockerel crowing. Usually when it is on, the boys get very rowdy and it's more interesting watching them getting into trouble. We all love Old Mother Riley. She is ugly and looks like a man dressed up as a woman. She wears a white cotton bonnet tied under her chin and long black clothes; all she does is shout and scream at her daughter. Mam sez she is a man and her daughter is her wife. I just can't work that out.

The boys' favourites are 'The Bowery Boys'. They are a gang of young American ruffians who live in the Bowery and are always in trouble. Still, they always turn out to be the heroes at the end of the film. The ones I don't like at all are 'The Three Stooges', they are very scary to me and never make me laugh. But then there are the cowboy films - Gene Autry, he rides along on his horse, always singing to a pretty girl. These are the days of romance, with a big R. When the hero kisses the girl, the boys all make loud noises as if they are going to be sick, and stamp their feet. They spoil it for us girls, we love those bits! There is 'Hop-a-Long Cassidy', and 'Roy Rogers' and his horse Trigger. My favourite is 'The Lone Ranger' and his horse 'Silver'. When he rides onto the screen in his mask and yells "HI HO, SILVER!", sending Silver rearing up on his hind legs, my little heart is beating fit to burst. He also has a side kick called 'Tonto'. He is a Red Indian. They are my heroes.

This is a time when Hollywood is at its greatest. The boys have all stopped playing soldiers and have now become cowboys. Not many like being the indians, so the big boys make the smaller ones be them, the same as they did when they were Gerries. It is no wonder they don't want to, they always have to lose. We girls like to be the heroines they rescue when they play cowboys and they have to grab us off one of the others. Sometimes, it's quite painful especially if they each pull an arm. We also play British Bulldog and Tag with them. They win most of the time, some of them are too rough but sometimes one of them gives you a quick kiss. I'm still not as popular as my friend, with the thick lisle long brown stockings which she holds up with elastic garters. I still have to wear ankle socks, even though I plead every day with Mam.

At the bottom of the street round the corner from us there's a grocer's shop, and if you are lucky you can buy a bag of broken biscuits for a penny. Sometimes, if you're very lucky, you find an almost whole one. If you find one with a bit of cream on you think your ship has come in, it takes ages to lick it off. When we are really well off on a Saturday morning before the pictures, we go to Brereton's, the posh fruit shop in Dalton Road. We put a halfpenny or a penny each together and for tuppence we can buy a bag of damaged fruit. I have to go in for it as my face seems to fit the best and I always get more than the rest. Lots of the fruit is quite good and most of the time we don't have to spit out more than we eat. Although the war isn't over, life to me is now wonderful. With lots of pals and these treats, what more can I ask for.

On one of the corners of our street is Lennie the hairdresser; my mam goes there. Sometimes she takes me with her to get my hair trimmed. I can't stop staring at him, he is a man but has lipstick and powder on his face and he is fat like a lady. He has a very soft voice and his hair is longer than I've seen on a man. Men usually have a short back and sides. Mam whispers it's rude of me to stare and that he's a really good hairdresser. When it's Mam's turn she takes her hat off and he sez it's lovely. I can't help laughing when he asks Mam if he can try it on. Mam gives me a look, which tells me to shut up. It doesn't suit him but I daren't laugh though. He's very friendly in the shop but never seems to have any family or friends. He never bothers with anyone in the street. It's strange really because when the grown-ups in our street sit out on the steps to talk and have a ciggy, he never does. I ask mam why a man would want to try a ladies hat on, when we left the shop. I have seen men mocking him and he seems very frightened. I ask her why they do that. She just sez he is a really nice man and it's a shame. I don't know what it is a shame for, and she doesn't tell me.

One day there's an ambulance at his door and Mam goes down to see what is the matter. She talks to the ambulance men and they ask her to lock up, and take him away on a stretcher. When Mrs Carr comes in for her daily cuppa, Mam tells me to go and play upstairs. I make a noise going up and then sneak down to listen.

I hear Mam tell Mrs Carr, "He's had a nervous breakdown".

Mrs Carr sez, "He had a really bashed face".

Mam tells her, "Some men have done it". Then sez "I don't know why they can't leave well alone". She then tells Mrs Carr the strangest thing is he has papered his living room with used five pound notes. They are big white ones and Mam sez it must be the most expensive wallpaper in Britain.

CHAPTER FOURTEEN
IT'S OVER

Mam's shaking me.

"What's the matter, Mam?", I can't wake up properly.

"Get up Jane, it's over! Can't you hear all the noise?". I think the war has started again, so start to have a cry.

"No silly, listen!", Mam is really excited. Then I hear it: bells ringing, car horns beeping, ships' hooters blowing, and the air-raid siren again – though we don't have raids anymore. I hear music and people shouting and laughing out in the street.

"What's happening, Mam?", I rub my eyes; I can't wake up and think I must be dreaming.

Mam's crying and laughing at the same time. "The war is over, over, the war's over!". She is so happy. I jump out of bed, wide awake now.

"Get dressed, you can come out in the street with Tom and me. This is a very special time. There won't be another like it".

It is! The street is full of magic, there are people everywhere kissing, hugging and crying. Someone starts to play an accordion, everyone starts to dance and sing. Mam swings away from me and I stand fascinated and in a magic land. An airman in his blue uniform grabs me and starts to swing me along with the dancers. I've never felt so happy and grown-up. We dance for hours. No-one is tired or hungry, just full of elation. The war is over at last, and everything is going to be OK. It's dawn before Mam puts me back to bed, she even gives me a kiss. I don't think any grown-ups go to bed at all this night. All they want to do is to listen to Mr Churchill on the wireless.

On 8th May, everyone in our town celebrates. There are bonfires lighting up the sky. Like thousands of others, Mam takes us up to the Town Hall. There are so many tall people there, I'm scared I might lose Mam. Everyone is so happy! They are all cheering, clapping and kissing. I listen to the bells ringing, and ships' sirens and hooters blowing again; watch the searchlights dance across the sky, listen to the bangs that are fireworks not bombs. There's a group of big boys going up and down Abbey Road banging drums and everyone has put lights on everywhere. It's all magical! Though still young I realise I am watching and hearing something that I will never ever forget. No one who hasn't witnessed this will ever be able to imagine it. We have a street party and everyone is out, stringing up red, white and blue flags, paper flowers in red white and blue are arranged around our doorways. I have no idea where people have got them from.

Mam tells me the flags are made out of white sheets, some are dyed red and blue then cut up. Tables are put up all down the street, people bring out sheets to make long table cloths and everyone manages to find some party food, egg and spam sandwiches, jellies and blancmanges, I hate blancmange! There are homemade biscuits not even broken, and lots of homemade lemonade. We wear funny hats that some of the women have made out of paper and a man plays his accordion. Someone has dragged a piano out, which they start to play. At the end of our party we all stand up and sing *"God Save The King"*. It's the most exciting day of our lives. At night, when they have cleared our mess away, the grown-ups play the piano and we all dance till we can't stay awake any more.

* * * * * * *

Things don't get easier though, rationing is still very much in force and food is even shorter. Mam sez Dad will be coming home soon, but he doesn't, not for what seems like a long time.

Someone knocks at the door. Mam's in the lav. I open it. There's a man at the door in Army uniform, who smiles at me. I don't like the look of him. He starts to walk in so I run for Mam.

She comes in and sez, "Bloody hell! Why didn't you tell me you were coming home?"

He replies, "What a welcome, kid", then they kiss each other. He sez to me, "Come here Jane, I'm your Dad, don't you know me?". Then gives me a big sloppy kiss. I don't like it - or him - at all, so I struggle away. After all, Mam has always told me not to speak to strange men.

He sez to mam, "She's turned into a bloody, funny little madam".

I don't know him, I just can't remember him, he isn't a bit like the Dad that's in my imagination. It's sad for us both really, and I am never, ever close to him again. I lost my Dad in the war. He wasn't killed, he didn't die, but I've lost him just the same.

When Dad finally comes home, the Army has supplied him with shoes, a Macintosh, Demob suit and Trilby hat. He is very bitter about the way soldiers have been treated after the war. He won't send for his medals, he sez they are just lumps of metal, a sop to the ordinary soldier.

Many men feel the same. Dad had served in the Eighth Army in Egypt and Italy. He had fought with Montgomery against Rommel in the Desert. He was an engineer in the war and had five large guns to take care of. He had a motorbike which he rode to each gun position, the guns were large and had to be towed to each position. They snapped one of their joints each time which caused a hazard to the gun crew. My dad designed a piece that moved with the gun. He was blown off his motorbike and had some time in hospital and was mentioned in dispatches, but because he never collected his medals or talked about the war to us, we never knew what for. It was only in later years when he talked to my son - his grandson - that I heard about it. Then it was too late to find out as he died. I don't know his Army number.

The Christmas after the war, I wake up to find my very own pot doll at the bottom of the bed. The only thing is, it is still night. I am in Mam and Dad's room, and they are fighting and screaming at each other. Mam's screaming at Dad, saying he is strangling her. I cry and tell Dad to stop. He tells me to "Shut up, you ugly little bastard".

I don't know what a 'bastard' is, but I don't like being told I'm ugly. It's something I'll never forget. After all, you always believe what your parents tell you. The reason I am sleeping on a camp bed in their room is because I have yellow jaundice and am not very well.

The next morning I am allowed downstairs to lie on the settee. Everything seems back to normal. I am so excited with my doll. My Nana has knitted me some clothes to fit it. It is the most treasured possession I've ever had, even though it pops into several pieces all the time. My doll's head, arms and legs are all kept together inside the body with a broad piece of elastic and metal bars that go into each joint. It means that when one comes out all the others fly off, I hug it so hard that it happens all the time. I don't care. It is the prettiest doll. It has a lovely face with beautiful blue eyes, a rosebud mouth and dimples in its cheeks. Its legs and arms looked like they have bracelets of fat, and it has a dimple in its bum. I really, really love it.

We have a chicken for dinner on Christmas day, but I can't eat it cos yellow jaundice makes the smell of food to make me really sick. I have to stand in the yard while Mam cooks it. I'm mad because we are allowed only one at Christmas with our food coupons. My first ten years seems to have been dominated by the war. I wonder what life is going to be like after it.

It has to get better doesn't it?

ABOUT THE AUTHOR

Hi, I'm Lilian. I live on Walney Island next to a small peninsular in the North-West of England, part of the Barrow-in-Furness district in Cumbria.

I enjoy writing, updating my blog and commenting on day-to-day life around me, and the world in general, and look forward to making you smile at some of my stories.

Find out more about me at www.wookeysworld.com.

Printed in Great Britain
by Amazon

22987897R10059